Just for Today

Just for Today

✦

For Women That Do Too Much

Mari Peck

iUniverse, Inc.

New York Lincoln Shanghai

Just for Today
For Women That Do Too Much

iUniverse books may be ordered through booksellers or by contacting:

iUniverse
2021 Pine Lake Road, Suite 100
Lincoln, NE 68512
www.iuniverse.com
1-800-Authors (1-800-288-4677)

ISBN-13: 978-0-595-40726-2 (pbk)
ISBN-13: 978-0-595-67827-3 (cloth)
ISBN-13: 978-0-595-85091-4 (ebk)
ISBN-10: 0-595-40726-9 (pbk)
ISBN-10: 0-595-67827-0 (cloth)
ISBN-10: 0-595-85091-X (ebk)

Printed in the United States of America

Dedicated to Angela and Blake

You have both given up so much in my quest to put life into perspective.
God has blessed me beyond belief with your presence and love. You make life
worth living and you keep me young and open minded. I love you both so much!

Introduction

Nobody ever said life would be easy, did they? But they didn't say it was going to be filled with chaos either!!!! Somebody could have warned us. I'm guessing if you have gotten past the title page you either already know you do too much or someone that loves you would like you to get life into perspective. I feel your pain. That's not to say I've experienced what particular event you are going through right now but I have been in enough of them to know intimately the feelings of chaos, hurt, pain, frustration, fear, anxiety, sadness, and confusion. The good news is I have also had the amazing opportunity to also experience the feelings of happiness, elation, appreciation, thankfulness, joy, and peace. I would go through all the negative feelings a hundred times over to experience the positive.

Let me tell you a little about what prompted me and qualifies me to write this book. Like many of my readers, my life has been far from easy (as a matter of fact another book is in the works about that life). As a child, I never spent more than a year at any school until my sophomore year of high school (no, we weren't in the military—just had an adventurous mother). I supported myself through my senior year of high school. My parents died ten months apart when I was 18. Since that time I have experienced being an unwed mother, loving someone with an addiction, marriage, divorce, losing loved ones to chronic illness, unexpected accidents, and plain old age. I obtained both my Bachelor's and Master's Degrees while working full time, being a single parent for much of it, and raising two wonderful children.

I have also experienced unconditional love, passion, thankfulness, an amazing drive for success, determination, forgiveness; will beyond my comprehension, and people in my life that I know were personally put there by God. I have been protected, forgiven, and blessed beyond belief.

This book was a result of years of my own focus in the wrong direction. I am guilty of being an overachieving woman, a classic type A personality. My career has always been my life—it came before my husband, my family, and my God. In my mind it was the only way out of the poverty life I was destined to live. I worked hard and rarely played. Everything I did was at maximum speed and maximum effort. It was always all or nothing with me. Don't get me wrong. I haven't given up on hard work and determination; I just have a little better balance now.

I looked at my children one day and they were almost grown. All of sudden my "baby" was 5'11" and looking me straight in the eye (he has since grown to an amazing 6'4" and still growing). I wondered what happened—how had I missed so much of their lives? How had I given so much to employers and so little to my own family? How had I missed so many sunrises and sunsets and conversations with those I valued most? Almost simultaneously, the company I was working for was downsizing. My job wasn't in jeopardy—as a matter of fact I was promoted. However, I watched thousands of employees leave the company. I watched employees leave that had given the best 30 years of their life to the company. Although I don't disagree with how the company handled this necessary downsizing, I became painfully aware that it really all came down to business and it didn't matter how good an employee was or how much of their life they had devoted, it was all about business, politics, and what was best for the company. I realized that I, like many others had given 12–14 hours a day to a company and when it was all said and done, I was as vulnerable as the next person.

That's when I knew it was time to make some changes. I knew I was a hard worker—there was no doubt about that. I thought to myself, "If I worked half as hard for myself as I do for my employer, how could I *not* succeed?" So, I left my job and started my own consulting business that provides training solutions to organizations (both large and small). I put myself in a situation where I had no choice but to succeed—I was a single mom with two kids and I wouldn't let them down.

When I have worked for other companies I have had no balance. When I am passionate about what I am doing I give it my all—and I am passionate about helping others to be more successful in their work. Although I went through the motions of being a good mom (went to all the necessary meetings, carted the kids to the appropriate events, made sure their clothes were clean and lunches made) my *passion* was my work. It was easier for me to succeed in that area—I knew what I was doing. When it came to relationships I wasn't so confident or successful.

Through the grace of God I have been able to make significant changes in my life. I now take my 6'4" "baby" to school and pick him up most days (his dad is equally active in his life). My oldest is finishing Massage Therapy School. I start most days on my porch with Bible reading and a prayer and I end it with interaction with my kids. I still work hard but I'm no longer too tired, busy, frustrated or overwhelmed to enjoy the ten minute conversations, the Kansas sunrises, or a good novel. I gave up a lot to get where I am today—mostly many years of my family. I knew I wasn't alone and wanted to help other women put their lives into perspective before they missed out on too much.

I hope you enjoy this book. Don't let the urgent get in the way of what is really important.

Mari

Just for Today

I won't be so hard on myself.

My, we are perfectionists aren't we?? If only we were

- Smarter, kinder, funnier,
- Prettier, skinnier, taller,
- More prosperous, more energetic, more athletic,
- A better mom, a better boss, a better employee,
- A better spouse/significant other, a better friend,
- Blessed with better hair, lips, eyes, thighs,
- One size smaller, three sizes smaller, five sizes smaller,
- More artistic, more analytical, more confident,
- Less demanding, less judgmental, less focused on self,
- More spiritual, a better cook, a better housekeeper,
- A better you name it…our lives would be perfect.

We are our own worst enemies.
Nobody has to criticize us; we are way ahead of them.

Let's focus on our strengths and accept who we are today.

Tomorrow we can get back to beating ourselves up, but today, let's relish in the fact that we actually have something going for us.

We are smart, action oriented, and loving. We can multi-task like no man on earth, have people that love us, and most importantly, if we want to change, we can. Let's focus on all the things we are good at and even acknowledge there are a few in which we excel.

Let's remember we are human and it's acceptable (and even expected) to make mistakes and not be perfect. Let's focus on the fact our creator made us this way for a very good reason and trust that reason will be revealed to us someday. Instead of wishing we were something we aren't let's celebrate who we are.

Let's not be so hard on ourselves…just for today.

I'll forgive someone who wronged me.

People can be so mean sometimes. It's shocking that we can treat others so wrong. Our human weaknesses allow us to do and say things we may regret the rest of our lives. Sometimes it's hard to believe people can be so self centered and hurt us so deeply with their words and/or actions. And some of those actions are absolutely unforgivable—they may not deserve our forgiveness or worse yet, they haven't even apologized and/or asked for forgiveness.

Here is an irony for you—people who hurt us don't typically spend near as much time concerned about us forgiving them as we do focused on how angry we are at them. Of course this isn't always the case—sometimes the offender loves us deeply and just gave in to human weakness or simply made a mistake. They want nothing more than our forgiveness.

Regardless of the intent of the offender, what do we gain by holding a grudge against someone? Does it make us a better person in any way? Are we so perfect that we have never unintentionally (or intentionally) hurt someone else?

We allow those that we don't forgive to control our emotions and actions and more often than not they aren't even aware of it. Why would we give them that power?

Let's be a better person today.

Let's bury the hatchet and get on with our lives. Let's not let them have that power over us anymore. We don't even have to tell them we forgive them. It's a decision we can make without their input.

Let's forgive someone who wronged us—yesterday or ten years ago…just for today.

I'll smile more.

What a priceless, inexpensive, wonderful gift a smile is! Smiles have a domino effect—once you smile at someone it makes them want to smile at someone else. It's free, it's easy, and the impact is amazing.

A smile literally lights up a room. I've read stories of people that were seriously considering suicide when someone smiled at them and triggered a new found sense of hope in their soul.

It transcends across age barriers, nationalities, languages, cultures, and lifestyle choices—it works everywhere. A smile is a smile in every language.

I'm astounded that God provided each of us a tool, built in, that costs nothing and has such a profound effect on everyone around us. A genuine smile is worth so much and is such an easy way to spread joy without saying a word. Like a disease, it's infectious—you can see it start to spread immediately. Unlike most diseases, it's a good thing—no antibiotics needed, just sit back and enjoy.

Let's smile today.

Need something to be happy about? Let's be happy we are alive and happy to have the opportunity to affect so many other people. Or how about being happy about our health or all the wonderful people we've been blessed to know.

The reality is life can always be worse. Let's find the good and smile about it. Let's watch as the smiles are returned back almost immediately.

Let's smile at everyone we see; the little boy down the street, the clerk at the grocery store, the people we don't care much for at the office, our spouse and kids, even the grouchy old person down the street.

Let's smile more…just for today.

I'll dream about going someplace I've never been.

A lifetime of disappointments and/or busyness can cause us to lose sight of our dreams. We get so caught up in the activities of today that we forget to dream about tomorrow.

Without dreams, we have no future.
Without dreams, we are just a collection of activities living day to day.

We need to dream.
We need to imagine.
We need to dream it before we can achieve it.
We need to use our creative spirits and visualize a place we've yearned to visit.

Let's dream today.

Let's find a quiet place, close our eyes and dream about a place.
Let's dream about a place we have always wanted to visit.

Let's envision the trip to getting there. Will we go by plane, train, car, bike, or foot?

Let's imagine what it looks like when we arrive.
Let's imagine how the people talk and walk and dress.
Let's picture ourselves walking down a road or path in this place.

Let's imagine the store fronts, the shops, and the landscape surrounding us.
Let's envision ourselves talking to people that live here.

What sights and places will we explore? What will we do while we are here—go shopping, snorkeling, sky diving, walking, climbing, partying, or just relaxing? Let's visualize ourselves doing and seeing all those things we've always wanted to experience in this place.

Let's dream about going someplace we've never been…just for today.

I'll celebrate the fact that I am a woman.

Sometimes it seems as though we get so caught up in living in a "man's world" that we forget how wonderful it is to be a woman. We struggle through the meetings dominated by men, the frustration with not being taken seriously or concerns about leaving to have children. We feel powerless and dominated, as if we have to work twice as hard as men to accomplish our goals.

We aren't privy to the decisions made in the men's restroom, locker room, or during the most recent golf game. All we want in life is the same opportunities and respect that men seem to have but it eludes us. We think they have all the advantages.

Today, let's celebrate the fact that we are women.

The truth is we have a lot more power and advantages in this world than we like to admit. We are a very special breed.

We are softer, kinder, and more compassionate.
We are better people managers and relationship builders.
We aren't afraid to express our emotions, our fears, or our joys.
We can multi-task better than three men put together.
We are able to purchase and wear a variety of shoes, blouses, suits, dresses, and jeans.
We can wear make-up to cover imperfections, enhance our good features and cover our not so great features.

They may not all admit it, but men look at us in awe because of our ability to give, to do, and to be the women we are. Let's relish in that knowledge. We are beautifully created and the perfect compliment. We are painted and photographed by men around the world. We are strong and capable and intelligent.

Let's celebrate the fact that we are women…just for today.

I'll learn from my mistakes.

Have you ever wondered how you, someone so capable and accomplished can make the same mistake over and over and over again and never seem to learn from it?

I'm amazed at my own inability to learn from my mistakes. Here I am, a teacher, a person gifted to teach others, yet I still can't make the connection that when I choose to eat chocolate and I choose not to exercise, I will gain weight.

Really, how hard is that to learn? I think I'm doing really well, and then I mess up and realize I've made that same mistake 100 times. I once heard that God continues to present us with the same challenge in life until we master it. I guess that means he's going to keep putting that chocolate in front of me until I finally make the connection. And I consider myself a fairly smart woman! Can you relate?

Let's master those challenges today.

We are strong, capable, smart women with strong wills. Let's actually learn from our mistakes. Let's take a hard look at our habits and repeatable behaviors and be done with them once and for all. Let's make the connection between cause and effect. If you think about it, by repeating our mistakes over and over, we are like someone that touches a hot stove every day and thinks maybe it won't burn this time. I think they call that insanity—doing the same thing over and over and expecting a different result. Remember, if we don't learn from our mistakes they will be presented to us again. Do you really want to go through this experience yet again?

Let's learn from our mistakes…just for today.

I'll dance (even if I have no rhythm).

There is nothing as freeing as dancing. God blessed some of us with more rhythm than others but it is freeing just the same.

Watch a child as they listen to music and have no reservations about the movement of their body. They just enjoy the music and move with it. They are happy.

Go to a local club and watch people dance. Often they dance in groups of three or four and don't even limit themselves to couples. Look at their faces. They are happy and free and spirited (okay, maybe some are a little drunk too). It's rare to find someone on the dance floor looking like they aren't having a good time (unless you are at a 7th grade dance, then it's painful). The blood is moving through their body, the adrenaline is flowing. They are having fun! Dancing makes us feel alive.

Let's dance today.

It's best to experience this with other people however; even if it's alone in our own bedroom it will still work.

Let's crank up the radio and dance!
Let's turn around and around like a child does when they dance.
Let's turn the music up loud and listen to the rhythm instead of the words.
Let's get lost in the music, whatever kind of music it is.
Let's let the music permeate our soul and consume us.
Let's close our eyes and not let anything else enter our thoughts except the feeling of the music.
Let's raise our arms, sway, swing, bee bop, jump up and down, and/or two-step.
Let's feel the blood flowing through our bodies.
Let's truly experience the feeling of being alive!

Let's dance…just for today.

I'll be thankful for the trials in my life.

Trials are just opportunities in disguise. I know it's hard to believe when you feel like your life is falling apart but it's true. Trials are opportunities to learn, to grow, to see things in a way we wouldn't normally see them.

Let's say you are on your way to work, you have two kids in the back seat that you need to get to daycare and you are late to a meeting. Typical day, huh? Then your car breaks down on the highway. Now it's definitely a trying situation!! How could any good ever come from this?

Let's see…maybe someone pulls over to help you and it changes your pessimistic view toward humanity.

Maybe your car breaking down prevented you from having a wreck two miles up the road.

Maybe it's an opportunity to spend some quality time with your children and focus on what's important instead of what's urgent.

Maybe next time you won't put off your scheduled car check ups.

Maybe you'll use the time to pray the first prayer you've prayed in two years.

See, that simple trial is full of opportunities—it's all in how you look at it.

Let's be thankful for the trials presented.

Let's trust they are presented for a reason. Let's accept that we don't necessarily have to know the purpose. Let's just make the best of it and handle the trials as an opportunity to learn something new. Let's trust someone "bigger" has our back and is watching out for us.

Let's be thankful for the trials in our life…just for today.

I'll smile at every child I encounter.

Ahhh, children—the ultimate in innocence, honesty, creativity, enthusiasm, and unconditional love. Do you remember being a child? Do you remember how you thought adults were right up there with God? They were so big and powerful and all-knowing. And if they took the time to talk or smile or wink at you, oh, you knew you must be special.

They must feel so insignificant being so small. Having an adult give them attention (and positive attention at that) just makes their day. There is nothing more special than the smile of a child (okay, well maybe the hug of a child). And the best way to receive a smile is to give it first. Every child needs to feel special, loved and important.

Let's take time today to smile at the children.

They are our future and our hope.

Let's smile at them as they drive by in a car.
Let's smile while we wait at a stop light and they are making faces (or picking their nose) in the car next door.
Let's smile at them as we see them causing their parents great grief in the store.
Let's smile at them as we wait in the check out line or as we walk down the sidewalk.
Let's invest in our future.

Let's make a child feel special, loved, and important—smile at them…just for today.

I'll take the time to see the beauty around me.

It's easy to get so caught up in our busy lives that we don't take the time to see the beauty all around us. We focus on the house that isn't clean enough, or the rain that is soaking our "dry clean only" blouse, or the wind messing up our hair, or the snow making the roads unmanageable. We see the weeds in the garden, the thorns on the roses, and the mud created by the rain. We see all the personality traits we don't like in others instead of the beauty inside them.

We see everything that's wrong instead of everything that's right.

Let's try looking past the obvious and seeing the beauty in everything around us today.

Let's focus on how fortunate we are to have our home and all the love we experienced in it.
Let's focus on the beauty of the snowflakes falling through the sky, each as individual as you and I.
Let's focus on how wonderful the rain sounds coming down, the smell of freshness in the air, and the new growth that can only occur as a result of the rain.
Let's not get caught up in the details and instead focus on the beauty in the garden—the awesomeness of plant life, the smell, the feel, the touch of the flowers.
Let's focus on the beauty of others—their heart and soul.

Let's see the beauty in everything around us…just for today.

I'lll hummmmmmmm.

Have you ever noticed that people that hum are generally happy? I've yet to meet someone that was humming and feeling angry. I'm not sure but I don't think it's possible to be angry and hum. There is something about humming that is similar to the effect of smiling. If you aren't feeling happy when you start doing it you certainly will in a few minutes.

I'm not sure how this works biologically or psychologically but it does. Try it. Having a bad day? Hum your favorite song. Better yet, hum a song from childhood that brings back good memories.

Already having a good day? Hum as you stand in line or as you stroll through your office building. Watch the reaction of those around you. They can't help but smile. It's infectious and you are having a positive effect on others without even knowing who you affecting. If you pay very close attention you'll notice others humming too as they walk away, it's contagious that way.

Let's hum today.

Let's hum in the checkout line at the grocery store.
Let's hum as we sit alone at our desk and as we walk to the next meeting.
Let's hum as we cook dinner and do the laundry.
Let's hum songs from our youth and songs from today.
Let's hum gospel songs, opera songs, and childhood songs.
Let's pay attention to people around us and watch their reaction to our humming.

Let's spread joy and cheerfulness by humming…just for today.

I'll imagine a world with no anger and no frustration.

It may be a stretch of the imagination but let's try to envision a world with no anger and no frustrations.

Just think of it…

Instead of the undesired hand gesture by the driver behind you; a waving hand and smile occurs.

Instead of the scowl of your co-worker you receive a heartfelt greeting and warm handshake.

Instead of being angry with your significant other for neglecting to run the errand you asked, you are thankful they made it home safely and blessed with yet another day to be in their company.

Instead of being angry with the person that "took" your job, you are thankful because it provided you an opportunity to do something else.

Let's imagine this utopian life today.

Let's take a deep breath when we feel the anger well up within us and blow it out instead of raging. Let's see everything as an opportunity instead of struggle.

Let's stretch our imaginations and see joy instead of anger and peace instead of frustration.

Let's imagine everyone on our morning commute as being happy.

Let's control our own emotions today and imagine what the world would be like if everyone else did the same.

Let's see all the situations in our life in a positive way.

Let's imagine one day with no anger and no frustrations…just for today.

I'll read a novel instead of self-improvement or news material.

As women who do too much we have a tendency to utilize every moment of the day and not schedule any time to relax. We multi-task all day and if that isn't enough, when we go to bed at night we take a copy of the most recent leadership book, news publication, or home decorating magazine.

We are on a constant mission to learn more, be more, and have more. We think the only way to get ahead is by filling every minute with activity and learning.

Well, here's a news flash for you—we are wearing ourselves out!

Every now and then we need to relax. We need to do and read something for fun instead of improvement. We need to escape from our extremely hectic lives and lose ourselves in a good story.

Let's find a novel to read today.

It can be a trashy romance novel, a funny, feel good novel, a suspenseful horror novel, or a dramatic, spiritual novel. Let's escape to the lives in the novel.

Let's imagine ourselves as the heroine.
Let's enjoy our escape and become one with the story.
Let's relax and not feel compelled to learn.

It's not wasting time, it's giving our minds a rest. Our minds need a rest just like our bodies need a rest. Let's enjoy letting our minds roam.

Let's read a novel...just for today.

I'll laugh…a lot.

Did you know that laughter is a stress reliever? When was the last time you just let it loose and laughed until you cried? Can you even remember?

Laughter has been credited for healing diseases, improving relationships, curing depression, and improving sleep—and there are *no* known reasons why we shouldn't laugh (unless of course you are recovering from broken ribs)! There are actually physiological affects of laughing that are not totally understood by science.

The best thing about laughter is it not only makes you happy; it makes everyone around you happy too.

Let's laugh today.

Let's rent a comedy movie and laugh out loud.

Let's rent a DVD of a comedian and get the affect of being at a comedy club.

Let's call a friend that is notorious for being humorous and have them join us.

Let's just change our way of thinking and laugh at all the things we would normally get angry about.

Let's pull out our high school year books and show it to our teenagers—that's sure to crack everyone up.

We aren't looking for slight grins or chuckles; we are talking about laughing out loud! If you have the gift, use it to help other's laugh today as well. Remember, it's contagious, a stress reliever, and good for our health.

Let's laugh a lot…just for today.

I'll plan my next vacation.

We are a group of planners and doers! We have to be to accomplish all we do. We had our wedding planned (including each little detail) at least ten years before we met the groom. We knew where we would be married, what colors everyone would where, what the cake would look like, and how the room would be decorated. We even knew what the invitations would say except for the one missing line (his name).

We plan dinners, events, and parties at a moment's notice. We plan projects that range from landscaping a yard to designing an aircraft.

We plan our entire family's dentist, orthodontist, doctor, and hair appointments. We plan our children's educations before they ever start school.

And we plan our investment portfolio and can calculate fairly closely where we will be at retirement. It's too bad we don't take the time to plan a vacation into that hectic calendar we keep.

Let's plan our next vacation.

It doesn't matter if its two months or two years away, let's plan it.

Let's make our vacation as big a priority as everything else.
Let's look at travel brochures of all the places we would like to go.
Let's set a date and create a budget to pay for this trip.
Let's conduct some research on the internet of locations and costs.
Let's schedule a meeting with a travel agent or look for vacation rentals online.
Let's list the clothes we will take and events we want to attend.
Let's get excited about the opportunity to relax and enjoy time with family and friends (or not).

Let's schedule enjoyment into our life and plan our next vacation...just for today.

I'll tell my loved ones how much I appreciate them.

We sure have a tendency to take people for granted don't we? It's sad to realize those we love the most are often the ones we take for granted the most. The small "extras" that used to mean so much to us have turned into expectations.

Maybe it's because we feel unappreciated ourselves. Maybe it's because we've just become too busy to notice. Whatever the reason, we have a tendency to stop expressing our appreciation for those we love the most. Then one day we look up and realize they are gone and it's too late to tell them.

Let's not let time pass one more minute before we tell our loved ones how much we appreciate them.

Let's make sure they know how their gestures and small acts are noticed and appreciated.
Let's focus on what is right instead of what is wrong.
Let's watch them beam with pride because we noticed the "extras."
Let's communicate what they mean to us and not assume they know.
Let's express how glad we are they are a part of our lives and how blessed we feel to be a part of theirs.
Let's express how we couldn't imagine our lives without them.
Let's tell them "thank you."

Let's tell our loved ones how much we appreciate them...just for today.

I'll buy myself flowers just because.

Women have a natural tendency to be givers. We give our time, our money, our friendship, free advice, gifts, and anything else we have. We often give too much and don't leave any energy or money for ourselves.

Women with families that struggle financially routinely spend their last dime on something for their children. We buy everyone in the house clothes, food, and extras without ever thinking of ourselves. Most of the time this doesn't bother us—until someone in the office gets flowers. Then, it just hits a raw nerve somehow.

We never *expect* flowers from our family but there is that part of us always wishing and wondering "why not me?" We watch as coworkers and friends receive flowers for special occasions (Valentine's Day is the worse!) and although we are happy for them, we are sad for ourselves. Why doesn't anyone send us flowers?!

Let's send ourselves a bouquet today.

Contrary to popular belief there is no law against doing something for ourselves. For no reason whatsoever, let's call the local florist and have a bouquet delivered. We are take-charge individuals, why would we sit around and wait for someone else to do it?

Let's have them sent with a card that reads "Have a wonderful day," or "Thanks for all you do." Enjoy them sitting on your desk or kitchen table. When people ask who sent them say "someone that really cares about me." Get the people in the office talking. And if you have a spouse maybe he'll get the hint. But then again, it doesn't really matter; you still have the flowers to enjoy. Take the time to smell them and enjoy their beauty each time you walk by.

Let's send ourselves flowers…just for today.

I'll love without reservation.

Sometimes the hurts and difficulties of our lives influence our ability to trust and love again. We are afraid of rejection, that the other person won't love us back. Or we are afraid of getting hurt. We may have convinced ourselves that we only have so much love to give so we hoard it and save it for "the right person"—those deserving of our love. Some of us save it as if it were a precious resource that we can't give away.

How silly of us not to realize that our love grows by giving it away. It doesn't matter if people love us back—the mere act of giving it makes it grow and expand. It's as if when we give love to someone they are then able to love another—it's a domino effect. When we hoard it, we kill it; it loses its strength and momentum by being stagnant.

Let's love without reservation today.

Let's discount all those fears and open our hearts. Let's love the child that lives down the street, the elderly nosey woman we see sitting on her porch watching our every move, and the person at work we've noticed struggling with life. Let's let our love grow by giving more of it away.

Let's love without reservation…just for today.

I'll treat myself to a pedicure.

Oh, my gosh, if you've never had a pedicure, you are missing out! As women who do too much, we are on the go all day long, every day. We run from one meeting to the next, one errand to the next, and one child's activity to the next. We are generally hauling books, planners, briefcases, suitcases, backpacks, and children in the process. If all the running around isn't enough, then we stick our feet in shoes that are too small, have an unnatural shape, and/or are three inches off the ground. Girlfriend, those feet are taking a beating and they deserve to be pampered!

Let's get a pedicure today.

We can go with a friend or just go alone.

Let's make sure to pick a place that has one of those wonderful massaging chairs to sit in while our feet soak in aromatic water.
Let's sit back and enjoy the chair massage as our feet are surrounded by jets of warm water.
Let's close our eyes while they scrub our feet and massage our calves.
Let's use the downtime to just relax and focus on the experience—the aromas, the bubbling water, and the feeling of relaxation.
Let's take an IPOD of relaxing music to listen to so we don't have to hear the sounds in the salon.

No worries, no guilt, no "to do's," and no cares—let's just enjoy the experience.

Let's treat ourselves to a pedicure…just for today.

I'll experience life through the eyes of a child…again.

Oh, the joy of watching small children play! Life is so simple and full of discovery. Everything around them is something to be discovered. They look, they touch, they smell, they experience life with all of their senses. They are enthralled by the simplest object—a pan, a flower, a rollie-pollie bug. They can sit for hours with a couple of crayons and piece of paper. Their imaginations are unlimited—no barriers or fences prevent them from "seeing" things and places. I sometimes think businesses should have a child on their executive team just to keep them thinking outside the box. Their love for learning is insatiable and their love for others unconditional. Children don't judge, they just trust and love without reservation. There is nothing like living life through a child's eyes.

Let's look at the world through child-like eyes…again.

Let's explore life and re-experience the pure joy of discovery.
Let's close our eyes and explore our surroundings through touch.
Let's look for the little insignificant details all around us.
Let's wonder "why" the sun comes up each day and "how" a simple seed can push through the earth and create vegetables for us to eat.
Let's imagine with unlimited boundaries.
Let's love others unconditionally, without reservation.
Let's open our hardened hearts and give others a second chance.
Let's experience the wonder and excitement of learning or creating something "all by ourselves."

Let's experience life through the eyes of a child…just for today.

I'll think about my purpose in life.

Isn't it amazing that we can spend years on this earth and rarely wonder what our purpose is? We can just go through life day after day with activities that fill virtually every moment and we may neglect to consider why God put us on this earth. Maybe it's just too difficult to consider what special gift we bring to this world—what sets us apart from others. Maybe it's too difficult to try to determine why the Almighty saw it necessary to create us, allow us to go through the experiences we have, and put the people in our lives that He did.

Today, let's think about our purpose in life.

I'm not talking about your "to do" list, I'm talking about your "calling," your special reason for being. Let's take an inventory of our special skills, talents, and experiences that are specific to us. Let's think about our God-given gifts. Maybe you have an artistic gift, a speaking gift, an organizing gift, a loving heart gift, the gift of compassion. You probably have many gifts. Let's think outside the box and ask for help from people who know us. Each of us has a purpose on this earth, a purpose only we can fulfill.

Let's concentrate on what that purpose might be…just for today.

I'll spend 10 minutes imaging heaven.

Do you ever wonder what heaven will be like? The bible describes it but it's hard to tell if the descriptions are metaphors or literal interpretations. It speaks of streets of gold and mansions in the sky. There are many songs and stories that allude to a place of wonderment and absolute peace and serenity.

I like to think of heaven as a place of absolute perfection, a place of total peace and unimaginable beauty; a place where nature is untouched by man and people are untouched by hurt. Maybe it's beyond our simple human comprehension to actually visualize heaven but let's take a few minutes to try.

Let's imagine heaven…

No poverty, no anger, no pain,
No sadness, no violence,
No wheelchairs, canes, or disease.

Let's imagine the joy everywhere we turn.
Let's imagine the absolute beauty.

Let's imagine the environment—are there flowers, streams, grassy fields, forests, little bunny rabbits?
Let's imagine the weather—is it warm and sunny or is there a gentle breeze or light rain?
Let's imagine the sounds—is it quiet and peaceful or are there children laughing and playing in the background?

Let's imagine the people here—all the people that impacted our lives; the teacher that gently pushed us forward, the neighbor that smiled and encouraged us; all those people that held the signs saying "Go this way."

Let's imagine our father and how it feels to be so close to him.

Let's close our eyes and imagine heaven…just for today.

I'll not worry about anything.

You and I both know that worrying serves absolutely no purpose. It doesn't fix the problem and it certainly doesn't make us feel better. It doesn't help anyone around us. So why do we continue to do it?

Why do we worry about the finances and how we are going to pay all the bills? Why do we worry about whether the new boss likes us and what he/she will be like?
Why do we worry about how we are going to get everything done today that needs to be done? Why worry about our health or the health of everyone around us?

We can't control most of those things so what purpose does it serve? Do we just enjoy torturing ourselves? And the things we can control (our health), we should be doing something about instead of worrying. Do we just like feeling bad?

Today, let's not worry about anything.

And I do mean anything. Let's not worry about the things outside our control and let's fix the things inside our control. We can't control the weather and we can't control other people (as much as we hate to admit it!). Let's control our personal schedule, whether or not we exercise, and what we eat. Let's pay the bills we have money to pay and set a plan for the rest of our financial obligations. Let's make the choice not to worry because it serves no purpose and is a waste of energy—energy that could be better spent controlling the things within our control.

Let's make the conscious decision to STOP worrying…just for today.

I'll notice my cup runneth over.

It's so easy to become overwhelmed with our lives, activities, goals and to-do lists. We continually wonder how we will ever accomplish everything that needs to be done. There are so many demands placed on us that we feel like we can never begin to meet them all. We become disheartened and focused on our need for help, for balance, for relief from this insanity that has become our life. It's easy to regret decisions, activities, and the demands our loved ones place on us. We can get so bogged down in the day to day requirements that we can't see the forest for the trees. We can't see all the great things really going on in our lives.

Let's notice today that our cup runneth over.

Let's notice how blessed we are to have the opportunity to impact others' lives. Let's focus on the positive of the situation instead of the negative.

We are blessed women.
We are blessed to live in a free society.
We are blessed to have children.
We are blessed to be able to see, hear, walk, and think.
We are blessed to be healthy or blessed to receive outstanding medical care when we are ill.
We are blessed with freedom of speech and freedom to worship.
We are blessed to have had as much time on this earth as we have.

Let's take the time to look at all we have to be thankful—every day is an opportunity to make a difference.

Let's notice our blessings and how full our cup of life is…just for today.

I'll drink 8 glasses of water…and stay close to a restroom.

We know we are supposed to drink more water but for some reason most of us don't do it. We always seem to have an excuse—"I don't have time," "It makes me spend my day in the bathroom," and "I need my caffeine" are just a few of the more common I've heard. We've become addicted to flavored drinks that do nothing for us instead of reaching for the drink that cleanses, hydrates, and heals.

The reality is we make the decision that drinking water isn't important enough. The only reason we don't drink water is because we choose not to—it certainly isn't because it's not readily available. Water cleanses us. It curbs our appetites and re-hydrates our skin. It flushes out the bad and makes us feel better. Water is a natural, healing element for all sorts of medical problems. And, it's free (in most places). Why wouldn't we drink water?

Let's just try to drink the recommended amount for one day.

Let's drink at least eight tall glasses or 4–16 oz. bottles of water today. You can get the free stuff out of the water fountain or pay for the bottled water—but let's focus on drinking today (water, that is). Pop, juice, milk, coffee, tea, shakes, and every other drink does not count. Liquor with water in it doesn't count. Today, we are drinking pure water. Let's imagine it cleansing our systems and plumping our skin cells. Come on, we can do this for one day. No cheating here, get a glass and fill it up. If you live in a desert state add at least one more glass to account for the climate.

Let's drink eight glasses of water today and stay close to a restroom to be safe…just for today.

I'll move with purpose.

Have you ever noticed those individuals that always look like they have some-place very important to be or something very important to do?

There are no slouching shoulders or shuffling of the feet when they come through.
There is no look of uncertainty or insecurity in their face.

They walk with their head held high, their shoulders back, and look like they know exactly where they are going. They move quickly, taking in their surroundings as they go. They look happy to be busy and seem to have an unending supply of energy. They personify the characteristics of a leader—quick, decisive, observant, and happy. They move with purpose.

Let's move with purpose today.

I'm not talking about rushing everywhere because you are late. Let's focus on our destination for today as well as for eternity and move with determination toward a goal. From the moment we get up until we go to bed let's focus on that purpose.

Let's feel the blood circulate through our hearts as we move quickly, decisively, and swiftly to our next destination.
Let's breathe deeply as we walk and notice how our energy seems to increase faster than we can spend it.

Let's hold our heads high, set our shoulders back and smile at others as we pass quickly by them. Let's take pride in all we are accomplishing today.
Let's stay focused on our goals and move quickly toward them.

Let's move with purpose…just for today.

I will build a sand castle.

It is so important that we not forget how to play. I'm not sure what idiot came up with the idea that grown-ups can't play but they were wrong.

When we stop playing, we start dying.

I can just hear the excuses for why you can't do this one. "I don't live by the beach" will be the top one. Here's another good excuse—how about "I don't like to get sand in my shoes?" The great thing about the world today is we can have virtually any product at our fingertips within moments. Fortunately for you, sand is sold by the bag at virtually every discount and/or building supply store. You can even purchase sand in colors (something that can't be done at the beach). Let's show the neighborhood we still know how to play.

Let's build a sand castle.

If there isn't a park or beach close by, let's buy a bag of sand, pour it in a spot in the yard, pull out a few kitchen utensils, get a bucket of water, and build. For some extra creativity we can get some colored sand from a craft store and build a really special castle.

Let's feel the sand as it pours through our hands, as we mold and shape it with just a little bit of water. Isn't it fascinating to watch how something can turn from no shape at all, and with a little water, become the castle of your dreams? Let's enlist the help of others. It's always more fun to play with others than alone.

Let's build a sandcastle…just for today.

I will go for a walk without having a destination.

I'm a "walker." Walking is one of the best exercises. It's easy on the joints, requires minimal expense, and virtually anyone can do it. Walking can get your blood pumping yet it's a great way to enjoy the company of a friend (and thus accomplishing two goals at once). Like most "walkers" I have my specific routines—paths, times, and days of the week for my walks. I have come to realize that many of us are so focused on the accomplishment of time or miles that we don't experience the beauty around us.

I have the pleasure of living in the country. The other day I walked down a familiar road but had a totally different experience than I normally do. For some reason on this day, I was without purpose and was therefore open to experiencing my surroundings wholeheartedly. It was so beautiful that I couldn't believe I had taken it for granted for so many years. If you don't have the luxury of the countryside, you can find the same kind of beauty at the mall, or on the side of the road.

Let's go for a walk without having a destination today.

Let's have no other purpose than to experience our surroundings.
Let's listen and look as we walk today.
Let's clear our mind of all the problems and concerns and focus on the beauty all around us.
Let's not focus on the accomplishment of the walk and focus instead on all that surrounds us.
Let's notice the trees, the flowers, the animals, and the people.

Let's go for a walk with no destination…just for today.

I'll attempt to count the stars.

Remember what it was like to be young in the summer, laying on the ground outside with friends and trying desperately to count all the stars? Of course, in the midst of it all you lost count because you were sidetracked with trying to identify the "big dipper."

Remember how small and insignificant it made you feel to realize the vast universe that surrounded you? Remember how it sparked your imagination to wonder if there were people on other planets or if the people in Japan were seeing the same stars as you? Just looking at the stars made us wonder and imagine and dream. And of course, our thoughts and discussions didn't stay on the stars. Counting the stars seemed to be a catalyst for deeper conversations—our purpose in the universe, how long we might live, where we would be in 20 years.

Let's attempt to count the stars tonight.

This activity is good alone and with others (although it's more fun with others).

Let's get some friends together, sleeping bags or blankets or lay in the grass or on top of the roof.

Let's count as many stars as possible and get sidetracked finding constellations.

Let's wonder if our friends and loved ones are seeing the same view.

Let's wonder about life on other planets or the purpose of the universe.

Let's let the conversation go wherever it will.

Let's wonder out loud what we will be doing in 20 years (okay, maybe 10 is easier).

Let's experience again the vastness of the universe around us.

Let's count the stars…just for today.

I'll make time for my hobbies.

We need hobbies. They bring us joy and you just can't have enough joy. The best thing about hobbies is that we don't even have to be good at them—we just have to enjoy what we are doing. The funny thing is it seems when we love doing something, we become naturally good at it. Whether it is writing, photography, gardening, running, bird watching, skydiving, painting, or playing an instrument, hobbies have a tendency to force us to use a side of our brain or a part of our body that we just don't get to use in our everyday work.

We need the feeling of peacefulness and relaxation a hobby brings us. Unfortunately, in our fast paced lives, we let the busyness take over and forget about our hobbies. We quit doing the things we truly love to do—the activities we can lose track of time with.

Let's put away all the reasons why we don't have time for our hobbies.

Let's pick up where we left off.
Let's enjoy the process of rediscovering those activities we love.
Let's experience the pure joy of doing something we love to do without worrying if we are good at it or not.
Let's schedule the time and make it important.
Let's use a different side of our brain today.

We deserve time to do what we love. Whatever it is, let's dust off the cobwebs, put away the excuses, and find a way to make it happen.

Let's make the time for our hobbies…just for today.

I'll make a list of places I want to visit, and then plan the first trip.

There are so many places on this earth I'd love to visit! Although I've had the opportunity to travel a great deal throughout the United States, I've never traveled abroad. Oh, I'd love to see the architecture in Italy, the sun set in Hawaii, and the animals in Australia!

Sometimes taking the first step towards a goal will set the wheels in motion toward progress. Making a written, documented list is that first step in this case. Many times we will talk about the places we want to visit all day long but we don't dare write them down on a piece of a paper. That's a whole new level of commitment. There is something about writing things down that somehow holds us more accountable. We truly need to quit procrastinating on this point. All it takes is a piece of paper and a pen (a crayon will work fine too).

Let's get a piece of paper and start brainstorming.

Let's get the wheels moving forward. Where are all the places we'd like to visit? Go ahead, let's list them all! Is it a location far off or someplace we can drive in a day? Let's list every city, every museum, and every beach we have wanted to visit.

Now let's prioritize this list. Where do we want to go first? Which places are closest and most convenient? If we could only pick one place on the list to visit and money were no object, which place would it be?

The next step is to start planning. Let's plan this trip? How will we get there? What will it cost? Where will we stay? What sights will we see? Let's get on the internet and research this place. Now, here is the big one—when will we go?

Let's make a list of places we want to visit and plan the first trip...just for today.

I'll learn something new.

My mother used to say that if I didn't learn something new each and every day of my life, I had totally wasted a day that could never be regained. She would say that everything in life could be lost except the mind—the odds were unlikely that one would lose their mind.

Mom stressed that an education was my only way out of poverty. I remember on rainy days when we were bored, we would pick up an encyclopedia and read whatever topic we opened the page to. She used to randomly ask me "What did you learn today?" It became routine at the end of my day to reflect back on the day and rediscover what I had learned. Sometimes it was something as simple as learning a person's name and sometimes it was as complex as studying learning theories and theorists. I guess its no surprise that my life has become consumed with learning.

Let's learn something new today.

The mind is an amazing muscle but like all muscles, if it isn't exercised, it gets flabby. Let's make a conscious effort to learn something new today—something we wouldn't have generally spent the time learning. Let's learn as much as possible about this new topic.

Let's start with opening an encyclopedia or a dictionary and finding a topic we know nothing about. Then let's research it on the internet and find out everything we can about it. Or, let's research something we've always been interested in but haven't had the time to learn more about. With the internet, we have an amazing opportunity to have information at our fingertips. Let's exercise our minds.

Let's learn something new…just for today.

I'll play with Play-doh.

If you have small children, you know the joys of rediscovering Play-doh. If your children are older though (or you don't have children), I bet you can't remember the last time you experienced the molding of clay into shapes and creating a masterpiece from nothing. I love playing with Play-doh. There are so many colors and things you can build and create with Play-doh. I love the fact that when I mess up or change my mind, it's no big deal. I can just smash what I created and start over. My "product" doesn't have to conform to the shapes and colors of practicality. There are no limits, no barriers to what can be created! It isn't just about the end product; it's about the process of getting there. There is something about working your hands and kneading the dough that is so therapeutic. It's no wonder kids are so happy.

Let's play like a child.

Let's head to the local discount store and purchase several different colors of Play-doh.

Let's get out all the cookie cutters, jar lids, rolling pins, and blunt utensils and go for it. Mistakes are no problem—let's just smash it and start over.

Let's experience the smoothness of the dough through our fingers.

Let's make a ball and see how perfectly round we can make it.

Let's build rockets and people and houses and new inventions.

Let's go back in time and dust the cobwebs off the creative and non logical side of our brains.

Let's invite others to play with us—Play-doh is always more fun with others.

Let's play with Play-doh…just for today.

I'll believe in my ability to achieve anything.

I truly believe the only thing limiting us is our own limiting beliefs. I remember the constant chant of my mom saying "you can do anything you set your mind to." She planted that seed deep into my subconscious and although it may have been slow to grow—strong roots were formed and I have accomplished more than even I thought possible.

I had a terrible lisp as a child and ended up with a career in public speaking and training. I grew up poor (didn't even realize how poor we were) and my parents died when I was 18 yet I obtained a Master's Degree and a successful career. I wrote much of this book while working 12 hours a day for an employer and being a single mom. I'm no better than you—no special skills or family opportunities. I just believe in my ability to accomplish whatever I set my mind to and trust God to take care of the rest.

Faith is a mighty thing. We have been blessed with more ability than we could ever know what to do with. We simply have to believe in ourselves.

Let's believe in ourselves.

Let's unlock the door to all that potential and make it a reality.
Let's get rid of our limiting belief system and eliminate the word "can't" from our vocabulary.
Let's give each other the positive words that will propel us forward.
Let's change our self-talk to be one of belief instead of doubt.
Let's not listen to those people that try to push us down and know that we have more power in our souls than we can even imagine.

The only thing stopping us from achieving our goals is that muscle between our ears.

Let's believe in our ability to accomplish anything…just for today.

I'll put as much energy into my relationships as I do my work.

I don't know about you but this is a tough one for me. Maybe it's because I can visually see the accomplishments of my work but it may take years to see the results of my relationship building efforts. Maybe it's because I have failed at so many relationships already and don't trust my ability to succeed. Maybe it's because I feel more qualified for my work than I do my relationships—after all I have the required education and experience for my career. Or maybe it's because work is safe and relationships are so unpredictable.

Let's focus on our relationships today.

Let's transfer into our relationships that drive and energy that we exert so effort-lessly into our work. Let's give our best hours to our loved ones today instead of to our work.

Let's demonstrate as much passion for our spouse as we do for that new project we just started (watch out boys!).

Let's put our energy and ideas toward building bridges with our teenagers instead of in a brainstorming meeting for product development.

Let's get excited at the prospect of spending time with our family and friends, making deposits in their emotional bank accounts.

Believe it or not, if you leave your job tomorrow, you will be replaced (and probably sooner than you would like to think) but your family can't replace you and they don't want to. Let's give them what they deserve today—our energy, passion, drive, and love.

Let's put as much energy into our relationships as we do our work...just for today.

I'll run a hot bath, light a candle, turn out the lights, and have a glass of wine.

Oh, I hope you are reading this first thing in the morning so you can spend the entire day looking forward to it. This is so well deserved and oh, are you going to enjoy it! Can you even remember the last time you did this? Maybe I should ask if you have ever done this for yourself. We all need a little pampering now and then.

Let's pamper ourselves today.

This will take a little preparation so if you have children; arrange to get them out of the house. Make a stop by your local liquor store and purchase the wine of your choice—go ahead, splurge. You might also want to get some bath salts that smell tranquil (you probably have some in the closet that someone gave you for Christmas two years ago). Then, prepare for heaven on earth.

Let's run a bath, nice and hot (unless it's summertime). Let's light some candles and play some soft peaceful music. Let's pour your glass of wine and set it next to the bath tub. Let's turn out the lights and lock the door just in case someone is tempted to interrupt. Now, slide into heaven...relax...close your eyes...have a sip of wine...wash all your cares away...relax...no worries.

Let's pamper ourselves by running a hot bath, lighting a candle, turning out the lights, and having a glass of wine...just for today.

I'll dream.

Remember when you were a little girl and your day was consumed with dreaming of the future? You dreamed of the man you would marry, the type of career you would have, how beautiful you would look in your glass slippers, and the places you would travel. Maybe you dreamed of inventions—new machines or equipment that would make life easier. We didn't place any limits on our dreams—everything was possible.

Why is it that when we grow up, we quit dreaming? Did someone tell us along the way it was a waste of time? Or did we just lose our imagination? Or maybe we are so afraid of failure that we don't even want to imagine anything anymore. A life without dreams is a boring life. It's a life without possibilities, creativity, or hope. All great inventions started first with a simple idea that turned into a dream.

Let's wake up that little girl inside.

Let's imagine the possibilities.
Let's think outside the box.
Let's dream big—way beyond our current comprehension.
Let's dream as if we were writing a fairy tale.
Let's not be concerned with failure or being realistic.
Let's dream without boundaries, without limits, and without fear.
Let's dream of far off places and amazing accomplishments.
Let's see ourselves in the dreams—traveling, exploring, and experiencing.

Let's close our eyes and dream…just for today.

I'll make a list of things I want to do before I die.

There are so many things I want to do before I die. First and foremost, I want to make a difference in the lives of others. I want to do things with my kids before they grow up—show them places and create memories. There are places I want to see, things I want to do, and people I want to meet.

I want to live life without regrets. When I'm 90 years old I don't want to be saying "I wish I would have…" When my time is drawing near, whether it be tomorrow or fifty years from now I want to know I experienced all I could in life. I want to know I was focused on the important and not the urgent.

Let's face it; we are all going to die someday.

Some will die sooner than others but it is the one thing on earth we can truly count on.

Let's spend less time watching television and more time on our life's goals.
Let's prioritize and focus.
Let's take thirty minutes or so to think and dream about our goals.
Let's start with a simple list of things to do before we die, whether that is tomorrow or fifty years from now.
Let's think about the places we want to visit, the things we want to do, the people we want to meet, and the goals we want to accomplish.
Let's think about the family member we need to forgive.

Let's take the time to think about our future and let's start with a simple list of things we want to do. Let's write as many items as we can, not holding anything back. Let's try to get 100 items on the list. No dates, no pressure, just a list.

Let's make a list of things we want to do before we die…just for today.

I'll turn off the TV and experience life.

Although television is one of the greatest technologies ever created, it is also one of the greatest distracters. Television offers the positive qualities of entertainment, news, shopping from home, and even opportunities to learn. Unfortunately, it's addictive, it prevents the family from interacting, it turns your brain to mush, and we've created a culture of children that require instant gratification and constant entertainment. There is so much of life we are missing simply because we refuse to turn off the television. It's as if we are afraid to actually interact with each other and experience life without television.

Let's turn off the television today.

For 24 hours, let's not watch it at all—no news, no soap opera's, no HGTV, no reality shows. Instead, let's experience life.

Let's play a game with our family members or take a walk in the neighborhood.
Let's read a good book out loud or call a friend we haven't talked to in a while.
Let's write that letter we've been putting off.
Let's experience life without television.
Let's imagine what our life could be like every day without television.
Let's think about all the extra time we would have if we did this on a regular basis.

I know this one is a tough one but we can do it and we will be better people as a result.

Let's turn off the television…just for today.

I'll make a list of all I have to be thankful.

We forget how good we have it sometimes don't we? We tend to focus on all the things that we don't have instead of all the things we do have. We focus on our problems instead of solutions. We focus on our failures instead of our accomplishments.

Can you imagine how much better our world would be if everyone woke up each day focused on everything they have to be thankful for? What if we were thankful for the opportunity to experience life's trials? What if we were thankful that at least we have a job (even though we think the boss is out to ruin us)? What if we were thankful for each situation bestowed on us because it's another opportunity to learn and impact someone else?

Let's make a list of all we have to be thankful for today.

Sometimes it's hard to get started—let's start with something simple like "I'm thankful I'm alive" or "I'm thankful for the sunshine." Once you get started, it will get easier. Let's see how many items we can get on our list—have a race with a friend and see who can list the most. Let's think hard and not forget anyone or anything that has been a blessing to our life. Let's express our thankfulness for our health, our children, our experiences, our friends, our family, and even our trials. Then let's share the list with someone close to us so whenever we feel unthankful they can remind us how much we have to be thankful for.

Let's focus on the things we have to be thankful for...just for today.

I'll read my Bible.

Some people read their bible every day, meditate on the words presented, and strive to live their life according to the principles presented. If you are one of those people, I commend you. Other people open the Bible on Sunday morning when the pastor prompts them and never really reads the passages before them; they just follow along as the pastor reads. Then there are those people that open the Bible every day to read but the words never actually enter their soul. And of course there are those people that open the Bible a few times a year either when it's a holiday or they have endured some crisis.

Today let's read the Bible.

Surely, we can take a few minutes out of our busy life to read a letter from God.

Let's pray before we read that the words will permeate our hearts and souls.
Let's experience it as the letter it is—written specifically for us by God.
Let's explore each word knowing it was a letter he took great care in writing.
Let's read the verses and ponder how they can be applied to our life today. If ever there were an instruction manual for life, the Bible would be it.
Let's start with Psalms or Proverbs.
Let's explore this one book that contains drama, documentaries, suspense, love, travesty, heartache, poetry, and action adventure.

Let's ponder this love letter sent specifically to us by our father…just for today.

I'll devote my day to making someone else's day more bearable.

We often get so busy in our own life that it feels like we are helping other people all day with no time for ourselves—we help our spouse, our children, our co-workers or employees. We go through life playing taxi driver, chef, accountant, maid, and who knows what else. We are so busy being busy that we don't leave time to make an impact, to truly help someone who is having a hard time. I don't mean writing a check to the homeless (although that's admirable), I mean taking our *time*, the most precious commodity we have, and using it for the sole purpose of making someone else's day more bearable.

Let's really help someone today.

Let's listen to someone that's hurting.
Let's mow the lawn for our elderly neighbor.
Let's buy a couple of sacks of groceries for a single mother.
Let's look that person in the eye that everyone seems to avoid and start a genuine conversation with them.
Let's pay for the person's food behind us in the drive thru.
Let's show compassion for another human being.
Let's ask someone that's obviously struggling how we can help them (and then do).

Let's devote this day to making someone else's day more bearable…just for today.

I'll live my life as if I knew I would die in one week.

Many people have struggled with the idea of their own mortality. Face it, the one thing you can count on in life is that you are going to die. We don't know when our time will come but we can be assured it will come.

What if you knew when your time was going to be? What if it was going to be in seven days to the minute from right now? What would you do differently today? What priorities would change? Would you be more kind and loving? Would you call someone you haven't talked to in a while? Would you enjoy a sunrise and/or sunset? Would you enjoy life more and work less? Would you forgive someone you've held a grudge against or help someone you haven't taken the time to help? Would you laugh more, love more, be more? Would you experience something you've always wanted to experience? Seven days from today could be your time. Tomorrow could be your time. We never know.

Let's live our life as if we knew we won't have another chance.

Let's quit procrastinating.
Let's focus on what's important instead of what's urgent.
Let's think of all the things we would do differently and then let's start doing them.
Let's tie up all those loose ends we've been putting off.
Let's enjoy this day more than we ever have knowing it could very well be our last.
Let's spend our time with the people that are most important to us.

Let's live our lives as if we knew we would die in one week…just for today.

I'll allow someone to help me.

As women who do too much, we have a tendency to want to do everything ourselves. We don't dare let go of anything because we don't trust anyone to do the job as well as we expect (not to mention the fact that we can't complain as much if we have help). We complain we don't have enough hours in the day yet we don't allow others to help. We tell ourselves and others that we would welcome help yet we won't even let someone carry a box to our car for us. We don't want to "bother" them.

We haven't yet figured out that helping others is a way to show you care. People care about us and they want to help. We are depriving them of an opportunity to show they care by not allowing them to help us.

Let's accept other's help today with a gracious "thank you."

Let's not let the words "no, no, I can do it myself" slip from our mouths.
Let's revel in the fact that we are loved and cared about.
Let's allow others to demonstrate their feelings for us. When they ask how they can help, let's tell them.
Let's not only allow other's to help, let's encourage them to.
Let's be appreciative and thankful for the help provided.
Let's accept help, graciously, kindly, without reservation, and with gratitude.

Let's allow others to help us…just for today.

I'll learn the names of three people I come in contact with.

It really is self centered of us not to remember people's names. We tell ourselves we just aren't good at it but truth be known, we just don't think it's important enough for us to remember. We don't seem to have a hard time
remembering our new bosses' name or the new VP in the corner office. We have
25 songs memorized but can't seem to remember a person's name we just met.

There is no greater joy than to have someone else speak our name. Think of
how a child, by about age two, can't wait to tell everyone his/her name and the
joy in their eyes when an adult repeats the name back to them. It makes us feel
important and valued when our name is remembered by others. And it makes us
feel unimportant and undervalued when other's don't remember us. There is
nothing more frustrating than to see the same doctor for five years and have them
still not remember you when you see them on the street. It's no different for
everyone else.

Let's make a conscious decision that the people we meet are important enough to remember.

Let's decide they are worthy enough of our attention to remember their names.
Let's learn the names of three new people today.
Let's make a point to introduce ourselves to a neighbor and hope they will do the
same.
Let's actually look at the name tag of our checker at the store or waitress at lunch
and say "How are you today (fill in blank)?"
Let's let people know how important they are to us by the simple act of acknowl-
edging and remembering their names.

Let's learn the names of three people…just for today.

I'll focus on my accomplishments.

We are our own worst enemies, aren't we? No matter how much we have accomplished today, this week, or in our lifetime, it's never good enough. We are a virtual punching bag—beating ourselves up over every little silly thing that didn't go just the way we planned. We always want to be smarter, faster, and prettier, have more money, have smaller hips, be a better mom, wife, employee, etc. When we lose 10 lbs., we just want to lose five more. We go to bed each night thinking about all we didn't get done instead of all we accomplished. Why on earth are we so critical of ourselves?!?

Let's take a different approach today.

Let's focus on our accomplishments instead of our failures.

Let's take an inventory of what we have done *right* instead of what we have done wrong. Let's shift the focus and write down everything we accomplished instead of everything we have yet to do. So what if the floor didn't get swept, at least the dishes got washed. We accomplish more in most days that some people do all week—acknowledge it and be proud of it!

If necessary, let's ask someone else to tell us our strengths and positive attributes. Let's look at our perceived weaknesses as strengths. Okay, so maybe our hips are larger than we like. At least we won't have a problem delivering babies. And it's a fair trade for a great smile and a healthy heart. Instead of focusing on what we need to change about ourselves, let's focus on what is wonderful about us. Let's view every failure as an opportunity—a chance to learn and grow. Let's see ourselves as the strong, independent, smart, caring women others see when they look at us.

Let's focus on our accomplishments…just for today.

I'll take a different route to work or home.

Change is good. It keeps us from getting stuck in a rut and acting old. Have you ever noticed that you probably have little routines you don't even realize exist? For example, you probably get up on the same side of the bed every day. You probably put your pants on starting with the same leg every time. You probably have an eating routine, an exercise routine, and a bedtime routine. We are creatures of habit. There are probably even people at work that know your routines because you rarely deviate. And I bet you take the same way to work each day. "They" say routines are important but I think they make us less flexible and adaptable. Next we become stuck in our ways, less open to new ideas and people, and eventually, downright boring.

Let's change something simple today—our route to or from work.

Let's not let ourselves get boring. Let's take a different road. There is more than one way to get to every destination. Let's pay attention to the difference in scenery. Let's notice the difference in the people and cars. If it's a residential area, let's notice the gardens and the hard work that went into beautifying this path. Let's time it—this new route may actually be faster. Let's enjoy this small and insignificant change in our life. Let's celebrate the fact we can adapt to this change.

Let's take a different path to work or home…just for today.

My only agenda item will be to exist—no to do's.

Let's face it; we need a break every now and then. Whether you like to admit it or not you are not super woman, you don't have to prove anything to anyone, and the world will go on without your contributions for one day. Employers like to make us think the place will just shut down if we aren't there. Everybody depends on us and we certainly don't want to let anybody down. Your "to do" items will still be there tomorrow and the company or home won't fold due to one day without your contribution.

Let's call in sick today—from work and from life.

I know if you're a mother you'll say you can't. Whenever someone says "can't," I can't help but wonder if they really mean "won't." You *can* do anything you set your mind to if you want it bad enough. Let's call a friend or enlist a spouse if necessary, but let's take a break today. No guilt, we deserve it.

Let's pretend we don't have a "to do" list.
Let's not answer the phone, wash the dishes, buy groceries, or even think about all the things we have to do.
Let's have no other plans for today but to exist, to breathe and take up space in the universe.
Let's wear our pajamas all day.
Let's enjoy just "being" and existing on this earth.
Let's not worry about anything and trust everyone to take care of their own "stuff."

Let's take a break from life…just for today.

I'll accept compliments with a "thank you" and a graceful smile.

So often when we are complimented we can't accept it. We absolutely do not know what to do with it. For some reason (maybe because we are so hard on ourselves) we think we are undeserving of the kindness. We think it isn't true. We think someone can't possibly believe we are beautiful, nice, smart, creative, fun, giving, a great boss, a great employee, or a great person. So, we take the compliment and either negate it with a comment like "no, you're the one who is (fill in the adjective)," give the credit to someone else, or say "are you kidding?" We won't even let people be nice to us. We steal their attempt at kindness by not allowing them to compliment us.

Let's accept compliments graciously today.

When someone says kind words to us, let's respond with a "thank you so much" and a gracious smile.

Let's really listen to what they are saying and be happy knowing we have made an impact.
Let's accept the credit for what we have accomplished or created.
Let's bite our tongue when we feel compelled to immediately reciprocate with a compliment of our own.
Let's hold our head high and not question their motive or sincerity.
Let's give others the opportunity to be kind to us today.

Let's accept the compliments with a gentle "thank you"…just for today.

I'll pretend to be a tourist in my own town.

We often take for granted the beauty and uniqueness of our own home town. We become accustomed to the sights and sounds. We stereotype the people and neighborhoods. We think we know all the stores in the various shops and malls. We run on autopilot as we drive through town, down the same roads we drive on each day and we don't even see the new and exciting things happening all around us. We drive right past people and landmarks and never see them. We long to get away, go someplace else and see different sights and people.

Let's pretend we are visitors in our town today.

Let's pack a camera, get a map and pretend we are visiting for the first time.
Let's visit parks we have never visited before or go to a museum we haven't yet explored.
Let's walk down roads we haven't walked.
Let's notice the design of the buildings, the landscaping and the artwork.
Let's pay attention to the way the sun hits the windows in the buildings.
Let's look at people and remember their faces.
Let's go to a little restaurant (not part of a chain) where we have never been.
Let's explore this town as if we were considering moving here.
Let's pay attention to the beauty of this town, the history within it, and what makes it different from every other city.

Let's be a tourist in our own home town…just for today.

I'll take 20 minutes to relax.

How did it ever come to this? How did we let ourselves get to the point that we have to schedule time to relax (and I'm not referring to sleep)? Why do we feel so compelled to do more, be more, have more? Why can't we say "no" and feel good about it? Why do we allow the pace of life to rule us instead of us controlling the pace?

Our lives have become so rushed and so fast paced that there is hardly time to breathe much less relax. I'm not sure we even know how to relax anymore. It seems when we have five or ten minutes to spare we are filling the time with thoughts of what we should be doing instead of relaxing—that's not relaxing. It's not enough that we fill in every minute of every day, we combine activities and for much of that day we are doing two or three things simultaneously. I remember driving to work while putting on my make-up and returning calls via my cell phone and sometimes even writing notes from the phone call at the same time. Not only was I a hazard on the road, I was a hazard to my self.

Let's take the time today just to relax.

No thoughts of "to do's", "shoulds," "wish I would ofs" or "what ifs."

Let's just relax.
Let's breathe deeply and exhale slowly.
Let's focus on the air supplying oxygen to our blood.
Let's consciously cause our heart to slow down and our muscles to relax.
Let's allow our mind to go to nothing but peaceful thoughts.

Let's invest just 20 minutes to relaxing…just for today.

I won't listen to the news.

I don't know about you but the news depresses me. Bombs, terrorists, rapes, murders, children missing—it's enough to make a person want to crawl under a rock for the rest of their life. Why is it that we thrive on hearing the bad things going on around the world? Does it make us feel better somehow to know that others have it worse off than we do? Or are we so desperate to have something to talk about with others that the news is all we can come up with (instead of maybe talking about what is going on in their lives)? Why do we have a need to have someone tell us the weather for the day when we can look out the window or step out our door and get a pretty good idea all by ourselves.

Let's not listen to or read the news today.

This includes the TV, radio, newspapers, and the internet. This could be tough for those news addicted individuals. If the news comes on the radio, let's turn the station. When it comes on the TV, let's turn it off. I'm not talking about forever; I'm talking about one day.

Let's just worry about ourselves today—not what the rest of the world is doing.
Let's try it for just one day. I guarantee the world won't end while you aren't listening and you know what—if it does, you can sue me.
Let's make a point to talk to people about what's important to them instead of talking about the news or weather.
Let's gear our conversations toward getting to know each other.

Let's not listen to any news…just for today.

I'll count how many people smile back when I smile at them first.

What an amazing thing a smile is! It literally lights up a room and can turn an otherwise awful day into a joyous one. I've read stories of people that were seriously considering suicide when someone smiled at them and triggered a new found sense of hope in their soul.

It transcends across age barriers, nationalities, languages, cultures, and lifestyle choices. We don't have to speak the language or understand the culture to share a smile—it works everywhere. I'm astounded that God provided each of us a tool, built in, that costs nothing and has such a profound effect on everyone around us. A genuine smile is worth so much and is such an easy way to spread joy without saying a word. Like a disease, it's infectious—you can see it start to spread immediately.

Let's spread some joy today.

We can do this while we are walking, riding, driving, or sitting in a meeting—we just have to be able to make eye contact. Let's make sure the smile is genuine—think about how fortunate you are to have this built in tool at your disposal. Watch the results of your smile. Let's think about the impact we might be having on someone's day. Let's keep track of how many smile back. Let's have a contest with a friend. Let's make it our Monday goal to beat last weeks' number.

Let's count how many people smile back when we smile…just for today.

When I feel the urge to strangle my teenager, I'll smile instead and remember how much I love him/her.

Teenagers are an interesting breed aren't they? Sometimes it's hard to imagine they actually came from our bodies. It's even more difficult to remember they have been in our home living peacefully with the rest of the family for over 13 years and now, poof, suddenly they act possessed. A plethora of questions come to mind when I consider my teenager. What are they thinking? Are they thinking at all? Have they forgotten they are not the only human beings on the planet? Certainly I was never like this as a teenager. What happened to those beautiful manners and that sweet child I remember a year or two ago? Who is this person and what did they do with my child?

Teenagers certainly try our patience.

Let's remember they are desperately caught in a state of limbo between child and adult and are tormented with which way to go. They are struggling with their growth, decisions, and future just as we are struggling with their moods. They are like a flower bulb just pushing through the dirt in the spring—trying desperately to bloom.

Let's take a step back and try to remember what a difficult time this is for them.
Let's give them our strength and direction, like a trellis to grow on.
Let's allow them enough room to breathe but not so much room that they take over the garden.
Let's provide our love like a spring shower so they can grow.
Let's give them our acceptance that will function as a fertilizer allowing them to arrive to their maximum potential.

Let's shower them with love today even when they are begging us to strangle them...just for today.

I'll forgive someone who wronged me.

People can be so mean can't they? Our human weaknesses allow us to do and say things we may regret the rest of our lives. Sometimes it's hard to believe people can be so self-centered and hurt us so deeply with their words and/or actions. It's as if they never considered the impact of their words or actions on us. And some of those actions are absolutely unforgivable—they may not deserve our forgiveness. To add insult to injury they may have never apologized and/or asked for forgiveness.

Here is an irony for you—people who hurt us don't typically spend near as much time concerned about us forgiving them as we do focused on how angry we are at them. Not forgiving them only hurts us—it doesn't hurt them. By not forgiving, we are giving them complete control. Of course this isn't always the case—sometimes the offender loves us deeply and just gave in to a human weakness or momentarily lost their senses. They want nothing more than our forgiveness.

What do we gain by holding a grudge against someone?
Does it make us a better person in any way?
Are we so perfect that we have never unintentionally hurt someone else?

Let's be a bigger person today.

Let's forgive someone who wronged us, yesterday or ten years ago.
Let's forgive them in our heart and not out loud if necessary.
Let's bury the hatchet and get on with our lives.
Let's remember we gain nothing by holding a grudge against someone else.
Let's not allow another human being to control our feelings any longer.
Let's not let bitterness and hatred be a part of us.

Let's forgive someone who wronged us…just for today.

I'll send an encouraging note to someone I care about.

We often get so caught up in our own "stuff" that we neglect to notice those around us that need our support. We ignore the man down the street whose wife died over a year ago. We vaguely listen as our teenage daughter goes through the drama of the week. We know our friend is struggling with her job but are just too busy to be there for her.

Doesn't it feel good to receive a card or note of kindness when life is a struggle? Especially when we are having a bad day, when we feel like the world has one purpose and one purpose only—to make us insane. There is nothing better than finding a hand written note of encouragement on our desk or in the mailbox. Better yet, it's nice to receive a note for no reason at all—just because someone was thinking of us or wants to encourage us to pursue our dreams. Those notes are the best.

Let's pay more attention to those around us.

Let's notice when it looks like someone is having one of those days. It may be the clerk at the grocery store or someone you live with.

Let's send a card to someone we know is having a tough time dealing with life.
Let's remind them that we are here for them, they can count on us, and as time has a way of doing, this time too will pass.
Let's acknowledge their hardship and tell them we care.
Let's remind them how much they mean to us.
Let's send a note to someone we care about that we haven't talked to in a while.

Let's encourage someone who needs it…just for today.

I'll pray for someone who hasn't been very nice to me.

Some people seem to live to make others miserable. They play mind games and it appears the only way to build themselves up is to tear others down. It's as if their purpose in life is to hurt others to bring them down to their level somehow.

When I was a kid I remember my mother telling me this was immaturity. As time moved on, I found adults play the same games, just at different levels. Sometimes for no apparent reason they lash out and so often it is on a day when you just can't handle any more lashing out. Once they realize you will take it, they seem to lash out over and over again, each and every time you come into contact with them. It's enough to make a person want to hold a grudge!

Just for today, let's pray for that person that hasn't been very nice.

Let's ask God to heal the hurt and pain that must be within them to make them act so angry. Experience has taught me that people generally act that way when they have been deeply hurt. Maybe they were tortured on the playground and see you as a threat. There is no way to know but let's pray for peace for them. While we're at it, let's ask God to give us guidance on how to help them. Let's pray for a shield that protects us from their unkind words and actions. Every time they lash out let's say a silent prayer.

Let's pray for that person that hasn't been very nice…just for today.

I'll call a friend I haven't talked to in awhile.

Friends are what make the journey on earth more tolerable, more entertaining, and more real. What would we do without our friends? They are the glue that holds our sanity together. Some of us haven't learned yet that life isn't about accomplishments, it's about relationships.

As busy moms, doctors, lawyers, managers, employees, educators, wives, we have a tendency to lose touch with those people that are such a huge part of our past, our memories, and our souls. We lose touch with the very people that have followed us in our journeys, guided us in the right direction when we struggled with the path presented, rejoiced with us in our triumphs, and cried with us in our pain. We allow life to get in the way of maintaining these very important relationships.

Let's call (or better yet, stop by and see) a friend we haven't talked to in awhile.

Let's put life into perspective and focus on just one relationship.
Let's express interest in their life.
Let's listen.
Let's meet for coffee and reminisce about the "good ole days."
Let's make sure they know how important they are to us.
Let's not allow busyness to get in the way of this friendship.
Let's make this person a priority.

Let's call a friend we haven't talked to in awhile…just for today.

I'll thank God for everything wonderful in my life.

It's easy to focus on all the things wrong in our life instead of all the wonderful things in our life. We get irritated by the driver going too slow that makes us late for a meeting. We can't believe its raining and we don't have an umbrella. We bicker with our spouse/significant other/children because they aren't doing what we need them to do. We have more to do than hours to do them. Our hair isn't cooperating today and can you believe we ripped another pair of pantyhose!!

Let's take a step back and think about all the good going on in our lives.

Let's thank God for all the wonderful people he has put in our lives.
Let's thank him for our health and the health of those we love.
Let's thank him for giving us wonderful children to mold and shape and love.
Let's thank him for all the conveniences we enjoy—the car, the radio, the coffee pot, a bathroom.
Let's thank him for the little old lady driving slow in front of us because she is probably protecting us from a wreck up the road.
Let's thank him for giving us the ability to influence so many people.
Let's thank him that we have hair on our head and legs to put pantyhose on.
Let's thank him for the rain to help the flowers grow.
Let's have a heart of thankfulness today.

Let's thank God for everything wonderful in our lives today…just for today.

I'll look in the mirror and see something positive about myself.

How did we ever get to be so hard on ourselves? So hard that we can't even see anything good? We see everything that needs to be changed instead. We see hair we don't like, hips that seem to get wider each year, and lines on our faces that weren't there yesterday. We see the gray creeping in and sagging skin that once was firm. How did we get to a point where we only look in mirrors from the shoulders up or worse yet, not at all? What kind of world is it that has us believing we should always look like we did when we were 18? If God intended us all to look 18 our bodies wouldn't age.

Let's embrace our aging bodies and take pride in the fact that we earned every single wrinkle, gray hair, and dimple in our thighs.

I'm not saying we shouldn't strive to be fit or that we shouldn't take care of ourselves. But we need to be able to look in the mirror and be happy with who we are instead of condemning ourselves because we don't look like the latest supermodel. Let's look at our bodies as a beautiful work of art created by a perfect artist—God. Let's look at ourselves and see past the aging body on the outside and right through to the beautiful person on the inside. Let's look past the "flaws" and see the good parts. Let's ask our men what they like best about us and believe them. Let's be happy with who we are and who we are yet to be.

Let's look in the mirror and see something positive…just for today.

I'll remember a wonderful memory from my past.

People today don't seem to focus enough attention on their good memories. All we hear about are people blaming their lack of success or their time in jail on their bad past. Don't get me wrong, I'm sure our past does influence our future to a large extent. We all have bad memories of our past. We all have times we would rather forget and definitely don't want to talk about. But we also have some wonderful memories of our past. Memories we cherish and never want to forget. Memories we hold close to our heart. We have visual images of a time long ago—a happy time in our life. Life is short, why would we want to dwell on times that weren't good and we can do nothing about? As adults, we have the choice to dwell on the bad memories or the good.

Let's remember the good times and good people today.

Let's take the time to remember the good—the times that have influenced us and the times that have molded us.

Let's remember the summer vacations, the family outings and the friends of a time gone by.

Let's remember our childhood and the exploring and pretending we used to do.

Let's remember the silly games we used to play.

Let's sit back, close our eyes, remember, smile, and be thankful for those moments, those people, and those places.

Let's remember those wonderful memories from a time long ago…just for today.

I'll blow bubbles in my skim milk.

Have you ever wondered why children are fascinated with blowing through their straw into their milk to make bubbles? Well, wonder no more…its fun, that's why! In a world where they feel powerless and have no control or authority whatsoever, they can control the number of bubbles they create in their milk. They can decide whether to blow harder or softer and learn immediately how cause and effect work in the real world. The can watch as their own breath and a simple straw seems to give life to a carton of milk.

Sometimes we feel like we have no power either. Worse yet, we begin to forget how to have fun. We feel like the laws of the universe are in direct conflict with what we want and need to achieve. There are days we feel completely powerless to control our own emotions much less anything else in the universe. And did I say, we forget how to have fun?

Let's blow bubbles in our milk today.

Let's get an extra straw at the drive thru, take it home and prepare to have fun. This activity is best accomplished with more than one person present. Let's surprise the family and/or spouse at dinner (or breakfast) and just break out the straw and start blowing bubbles in our milk. I don't care how old your kids are—they will think this is funny. If you are fortunate enough to have small children present make a contest of it—they will learn that we too know how to have fun. Better yet, let's sit at McDonalds and blow bubbles in front of everyone else. Let's see if we can get other people to join us.

Let's blow bubbles in our skim milk…just for today.

I'll refrain from screaming at someone who really deserves it.

It seems like some people are just begging for someone to scream at them. They push and push us to the absolute limit of our patience. They do stupid things that anyone with a brain should know better than to do. And they appear to have planned their day around irritating others. They are taunting, seeing how long it will take before you explode. Is it really possible that people plan their days around frustrating others? It's as if they are playing a mental game with us to see how long it takes to explode.

Let's not let them get to us today.

Let's not let them win.
Let's throw them off balance and just smile at them as they "beg us to scream at them."
Let's take a deep breath and realize that in the scope of life what they are doing right now is not that significant.

Let's imagine them naked (okay well, maybe that will make us scream—you'll have to use your own discretion with that idea).
Let's imagine them with a bobble head performing interesting animations.
Let's imagine replaying their actions and words backward.

Let's say a silent prayer for them instead of screaming at them.
Let's take solace in knowing we are in control of our emotions so even though they really deserve it, we aren't going to lower ourselves to that behavior.

Let's refrain from screaming at someone that really deserves it...just for today.

I'll remember I can single-handedly make a difference…and do something.

There are so many people out there that single-handedly made a tremendous impact on my life—I mean life altering impact. My brother, who saved me from my own self-destruction and made me want to be a better person. Various teachers that somehow convinced me I had the potential to be so much more that where I came from and friends too numerous to count. Then there are the acquaintances in my life—some of which I never even knew their names. There were those that made a difference in one day simply by caring—by smiling or listening or offering an encouraging word. There were those that made a difference in my viewpoint of humanity based on a single act of kindness. There are people I have never met that have said or done something I've remembered ten years later. I don't know if those people knew or planned to make a difference but they did. They single-handedly altered the direction of my life.

Let's make a difference.

Let's make a difference through random acts of kindness.
Let's actually visit with our children's friends and be interested in their lives.
Let's smile and wave at others during our morning commute instead of honking and talking on our cell phone.
Let's encourage the clerk at the store to pursue her dreams.
Let's help a child at the local grade school learn to read.
Let's listen when someone needs to talk.
     We can do it with a smile. We can do it by caring. Let's actually do more than talk about it—let's do something.

Let's make a difference today in someone's life…just for today.

I'll smell the flowers.

It seems so simple doesn't it, almost cliché? But how often do we walk right past rows and rows of flowers and never take the five seconds to bend over and smell them. We rush, rush, rush—here, there, and everywhere. Virtually everything becomes more important than taking the time to smell the flowers. We look past the gift God provided for our day, rush right past it in all the busyness of our lives.

There is nothing like the smell of flowers. Their fragrance and beauty are rarely outdone. So fragrant are they that a complete line of products have been patterned with their scent—bath products, hand lotion, candles, shampoo, and potpourri are just a few of those items.

Did you know our sense of smell can affect our moods, our ability to relax, and our stress level? Hence, the reason for the study of aromatherapy. In spite of all this knowledge, we still manage to stay in such a rushed state that we don't even take the time to stop and smell these beautiful flowers.

Let's slow down today.

Let's stop the crazy pace today. Let's take two seconds to notice the flowers and then another five to actually smell them. No flowers? Let's go to the local florist shop—believe it or not, flowers are available all year long. Breathe in deep, it's good for your stress and it's good for your nose. Let's not get so caught up in "activities" that we lose sight of what's really important. Let's enjoy the benefits of natural aromatherapy.

Let's slow down enough to smell the flowers…just for today.

I'll spin around in circles with my arms outstretched.

Do you remember playing at the playground or in your yard as a child? When we were tired of the traditional toys (or there weren't any), we'd resort to spinning round and round in circles as fast as we could. I would look up to the heavens and go as fast as I could go with my arms outstretched and wondering if I went fast enough, could I fly? For some reason I found this activity amazingly humorous because I remember laughing so hard it would make me fall down.

I've noticed many other children in this activity and wondered why they enjoy it so much. So, I started thinking about it and tried it again as a "grown up." Here's what I found out. I'm more easily nauseated now than I was then but if I get past that, the spinning is equal to a profound sense of freedom. It also provides a very different perspective of life. When you are spinning, the world looks totally different and we control the view. For a child, control is very limited so this is a very appealing thought. What I love about seeing a child spin is they appear "open" to whatever life has to offer and have no cares in the world.

Let's go outside, stretch out our arms and spin in circles.

In this life filled with meetings, deadlines, and barriers, we need to experience that feeling of complete openness and freedom every now and then.

Let's experience the feeling of having no cares whatsoever—just absolute freedom.
Let's enjoy the absolute freedom of this child-like activitiy.
Let's take a look at life from a different perspective.
Let's open our arms to the sky, look up, spin around and around and laugh out loud as we get dizzy and fall to the ground.

Let's spin around in circles and enjoy our freedom…just for today.

I'll take a good look at my backside and be happy with what I see.

I don't know about you but this will be the toughest thing out of this entire book for me to accomplish. I don't think I have ever personally met a woman that was happy about the way her butt looks. It's too big, too flat, not perky enough, too round, not round enough, nonexistent, or is the first thing you see. You know who did this to us don't you? It's the great marketing effort to make us crazy. You know as well as I do that they even airbrush the models images in magazines and yet we still hold ourselves to an unreasonable standard. For one day and one day only we are going to change all that.

Let's take a look in the mirror, a full length mirror.

I know this is tough and I'm there for you in spirit. Now, let's turn on the light (you thought you were going to get away with something didn't you?). If you can't imagine this without clothes at least wear something that is snug (no oversized shirts and baggy sweats allowed). Now let's turn around and face our backside to the mirror. If you don't have a full length mirror get a chair and stand on it. Come on now, on the count of three, let's turn our heads and take a look at our backside in all its glory.

You should be proud of that thing girl! Look what you had to endure to get that butt!! Nobody expects you to look like a supermodel but you. When your husband walks by and gives it a little slap, stand proud knowing that's his sign that he still likes it.

Let's put our shoulders back, stand tall, and be happy with the view of our backside…just for today.

I'll take a nap.

Z

Z

Z

Z

Z

Z

Z

Z

Z

Z

Z

We deserve it. Let's take a nap…just for today.

I'll read poetry.

I confess I'm not a poetry reader. I *want* to read poetry and of course I have a few favorite poems but all in all, I find it difficult to sit down and read Robert Frost or Emily Dickenson. I even have books on each but it takes a special day and mood for me to get those books out. After years of frustration with my inability to really enjoy reading poetry, I finally determined why it is I struggle so much.

Reading poetry requires a focused mind—a mind that is trained to catch the metaphors and play on words. Poetry isn't something I can read with the TV on in the background or kids running through the house. It also isn't something I can do while cleaning the house, talking on the phone, or planning the 15 other activities I need to accomplish for the day. For me, the untrained poetry reader, it's like reading another language—a beautiful language that flows eloquently and masterfully yet requires my complete attention to hear the "message." I avoid it because it doesn't allow me the opportunity to multi-task.

Let's read poetry today.

Let's find a quiet place where we won't be interrupted or distracted.
Let's let our mind go and place all energy on reading these passages.
Let's focus on how beautifully the author has arranged the words.
Let's consider the state of mind of the author and what he/she was feeling when this poem was written.

Let's get out a thesaurus if necessary to help us understand the language.
Let's read the verses over and over again until we "get it."
Let's get someone to help us that is experienced in this area.

Let's get outside our comfort zone (or just enjoy some leisure reading) and read poetry…just for today.

I will send flowers to a friend.

Doesn't it feel wonderful to have a delivery person show up on your doorstep or your office with a bouquet of flowers?! It's especially nice when there isn't a special occasion—no birthday, anniversary, or "Honey, I'm sorry I messed up" occasion. There is no comparison to the feeling of receiving flowers unexpectedly.

Flowers can turn a "blah" day where we'd be happier under the covers into a "life is wonderful" day. Somehow a bouquet has the amazing ability to make us feel special, important, thought of, and appreciated. There is nothing like that feeling. The best thing about it is not only do we feel special when we first receive them, we feel special every single time somebody else notices them. It's like getting a "you are special" card all day long.

Let's send a friend some flowers today for no reason.

Let's give someone else the opportunity to have a "wonderful" day in spite of life's circumstances.
Let's pick a beautiful bouquet that is sure to "pick them up."
Let's do one small thing to help someone else have the best day possible.
Let's help a friend feel special, appreciated, and important today for no apparent reason.
Let's write on the card how much we value and enjoy their friendship.
Let's turn someone's day into a wonderful day of surprise.

Let's send flowers to a friend…just for today.

I'll appreciate where I am right now.

I don't know about you but I always seem to want to be somewhere I'm not in life. I either want to have a different position, work for a different company, have a different home, be a smaller size, know more about a particular topic, live in a different state, and basically be anywhere but where I am right now. As I'm sure my ex-husband would gladly testify I'm never satisfied.

The good news is I'm learning. I've learned over the years that although it's very important to dream and strive to be our best, every now and then we need to be happy with where we are today. We can't be happy with anything if we can't be happy with ourselves. We are where we are for a very important reason—a reason we may not understand now, but a reason nonetheless. While working toward where we want to be, we have to somehow find a way to appreciate how far we've come and be happy with whom and where we are right now.

Let's take the time to appreciate where we are right now.

We've come a long way haven't we?! We've accomplished so much! We've matured. We've become wiser and more graceful somehow. We never expected life to be so full. Let's take solace in the fact that there is a reason we are where we are right now. There is a good reason. God has a perfect plan and although we haven't reached our destination, the journey is amazing. Let's be thankful for all that we have and all that we've become. Let's be proud of who we've become!

Let's take time to appreciate where we are right now…just for today.

I'll walk barefoot in the rain.

Rain signifies renewal, replenishment, and a fresh start. When it rains, a kid with no energy whatsoever will immediately become energized. You can almost see the flowers push through the earth and reach for the rain drops. The trees and bushes seem to stand taller, reaching for the droplets coming down. The smell of a gentle spring rain is one of those experiences we savor yet take for granted.

Unfortunately, we are so busy we have a tendency to respond to rain sarcastically with a comment like "oh great, it's raining." It means a mess to us because we anticipate everyone walking in the house with muddy feet. We see extra laundry and extra work. We see our hair being unmanageable and our dress shoes needing polished. We think we don't have time to enjoy the rain from our front porch much less go out in it. We're so caught up in the doing that we forget about the "experiencing." If we allow it, rain invigorates, gives us moisture, cleans the earth, and cleans our souls.

Let's take our shoes off and go outside the next time it rains.

Let's "experience" the rain instead of tolerate it.
Let's feel the mud between our toes.
Let's jump in a giant puddle.
Let's feel everything about the experience—the smells and the drops hitting our head.
Let's invite our husbands and kids too—it's not going to kill them to get wet.
Let's watch how happy they are when they play in the rain.
Let's stick out our tongue and catch a few drops.

Let's walk barefoot in the rain…just for today.

I'll treat myself to Chocolate without Guilt.

I admit I have a love/hate relationship with chocolate. Most of my life has been a constant battle with food in general, chocolate being the greatest sin of all. Unfortunately, the marketing experts of this world have become very adept at feeding my "sin" and making it nearly impossible to deny myself the occasional pleasure of chocolate. So, I give in, eat it—sometimes so quickly I can't taste it, and then the guilt sets in.

Oh, the guilt…I start beating myself up verbally and physically almost before the indulgence hits my stomach. It's as if I can see the chocolate move from my lips to my hips. I tell myself all the negative self-talk I can possibly conjure up. By the time its all said and done, I'm miserable for having "indulged."

Just for today, let's treat ourselves to chocolate without guilt.

We can feel guilty tomorrow. Today, let's enjoy every bite. Let's plan on eating the chocolate instead of buying it on impulse and hiding in the closet to choke it down before anyone sees. As long as we're planning on it, let's make sure it is "good" chocolate. The way I see it, if we are going to indulge let's make it worthwhile. Let's smell it as we take it out of the wrapper. Let's eat is slowly, savoring the textures and taste. We are talking about one piece of chocolate here not an entire box—it isn't going to kill you. It's a decision you know—what we think about and how we interpret our feelings.

Let's decide to eat chocolate and not feel guilty about it…just for today.

I'll take a Road Trip.

I know you are busy and there aren't enough hours in the day. I know life is hectic and your weekends are filled with cleaning, running errands, and taking kids to activities. But let's think about this. When you're dead, nobody is going to remember how clean your house is or what errands you ran on the weekend. Is it really going to matter if you dust this weekend? Will it be the end of the world if Johnny or Susie misses one soccer practice? If the bathroom doesn't get cleaned today, you can rest assured it will still be there tomorrow.

Let's pack the family in the car and take a road trip.

You can be guaranteed it will more likely be remembered than the fact there was no dust on the shelves. Do something spontaneous for a change—something not listed in your planner or on your "to do" list. Life is short—nobody cares if the house is clean but you.

Let's explore our surroundings and go someplace we've never been.
Let's throw a couple of fishing poles in the trunk.
Let's drive with no destination.

Let's not bring portable TV's, IPODS, Computers, or MP3 players—it's an opportunity to talk and experience an adventure together.
Let's teach the kids some travel games.

Let's pack a lunch or stop at some funky place along the way.
Let's just get out and do something together besides work.

Let's take a road trip…just for today.

I'll tell someone they are beautiful.

If you've ever talked to all those women you see that you think are absolutely beautiful you'll find that a large percentage of them don't find themselves very pretty at all. Even those people you see every day that you envy because they have great hair, eyes, figure—they don't necessarily feel the same way about themselves. We all have insecurities, even those people that appear to be totally self-confident.

The bigger issue here is how we view beauty. Why is it that *beautiful* to most of us only applies to the physical attributes one portrays? Why is it so hard for us to look past the physical beauty and see the real beauty within a person? What has happened to us when as a society we say the most beautiful person in the room is the one that most closely resembles a super model? And why does it not feel like a compliment to us when someone tells us we are beautiful on the inside?

Let's do two things today.

First, let's tell someone today they "look" beautiful. Let's make sure to do this as early in the day as possible so they have the benefit of feeling beautiful the entire day. Let's be sincere and even if you think they already know it, say it anyway.

Secondly, let's look beyond the physical beauty of others and seek to find their real inner beauty. Sometimes you'll find those that don't have the physical attributes the world seems to cherish are the most beautiful people in the world if you'll take time to "see" them on a different level. Let's take the time to find that beauty within others and acknowledge it. It is so much more difficult to be a beautiful person on the inside than it is on the outside—it takes more time, energy, and effort and it is so much more worthwhile. Let's tell these people how beautiful they are too.

Let's tell someone (or a couple of people) they are beautiful…just for today.

I'll encourage someone to pursue their dreams.

I envy those people that are naturally encouraging. You know who I'm talking about, those people that are constantly encouraging every one around them. They always seem to know just the right thing to say and people love to be around them. Hmmm, I wonder why.

We all need encouragement. God put more than one person on the earth so we could help each other out in a variety of ways. As I have to remind myself every now and then (more than I like to admit), it is NOT all about me. Even those people we think have it all together have doubts in their ability to achieve their dreams. They reach low times, they doubt their abilities, and they struggle with insecurity every now and then.

Let's put our own issues on the back burner today.

We can pick them back up tomorrow and worry ourselves to death. Today, let's focus our energy on encouraging someone else. I'm not talking about a two second "you can do it" statement. I'm talking about really encouraging and inspiring another human being. Let's spend time finding out what they truly hope to do and then help them think through their plan for getting there (not to be confused with planning their future for them).

Let's get excited for them.
Let's provide some encouraging quotes or verses.
Let's make sure they are fully convinced you are their cheerleader in this endeavor.
Let's push them gently.
Let's listen a lot.

Let's encourage someone to pursue their dreams…just for today.

I will not get angry or upset.

I have tried so hard throughout the years to be "peaceful" but anger seems to be a demon of mine I just can't seem to control. Therein is the problem—"control." That is why we get angry isn't it—because we can't control what we think others were supposed to or not supposed to do? Or could it be because we can't control our own impulses, behaviors, or moods? I've often wondered if my propensity for anger comes from just being the passionate person that I am—every feeling I have seems to be ten times more intensified than the average person. If I look deep inside however, I know that's a cop out. We may not be able to control what everyone else is doing (or not) but anger is an emotion we can control.

Let's control our anger today.

Don't try to sugar coat it by saying something like, "I'm not angry, I'm just perturbed" or "I'm just annoyed that's all." We all know what anger looks like—it's ugly, unnecessary, and generally serves to hurt instead of help. Whenever you get irritated today that someone didn't do what you asked or did do something they shouldn't have—instead of thinking about controlling their actions, think about controlling your own. You have a choice today—you can choose to get angry or you can choose to remain calm. I guarantee whatever crisis comes your way today is going to be better handled by someone in a calm state of mind rather than an angry, anxious, annoyed, or irritated state of mind. Let's make the conscious choice today to take control of our own mental state.

Let's not get angry...just for today.

I'll experience the beauty of the sunrise.

When was the last time you really watched the sunrise? I don't mean the sun was rising as you were driving to work. Or you were just getting home from a late night from who knows where and noticed it was becoming daylight? I'm talking about really experiencing the awesomeness of the rising sun. Could it be another simple act we all take for granted? We'd rather sleep, we're too busy getting the kids ready for school, busy, busy, busy or snoring, snoring, snoring.

How could we possibly take this visual awakening of the earth so for granted? What a beautiful sight it is to watch the sun as it awakens us with its gentle light and warmth! It's like a visual gift from God each and every day—a reminder of sorts. I can almost hear Him saying "Wake up child. I am here and I give you this day to enjoy." I think I am closest to heaven during the sunrise. It makes me think it is a glimpse of what is to come. I've been fortunate to see sunrises in a variety of locations throughout the United States and it amazes me how it can look so different yet still so beautiful from each and every location. How could we possibly think our business or sleep is more important than the gentle "Good morning" from our Father?

Let's check the news and find out when the sun is scheduled to rise tomor-row.

Isn't it amazing that someone can tell us exactly when this "show" is going to occur?

Let's plan for it.
Let's be there to say "Good morning."
Let's not miss this amazing light show.
Let's be early.
Let's brew our coffee and take it outside.
Let's pick a great location (I used to love to get on my roof).
Let's watch it rise slowly and gently with colors too magnificent to describe.

Let's experience the awesomeness and beauty of a sunrise…just for today.

I'll volunteer at a shelter.

It's very easy to grumble about all the things wrong in our lives isn't it? The house is messy, the kids don't do what we want them to, the spouse watches television all evening, the car needs work…you get the idea. Even if we are typically positive people, we seem to be focusing on the negative in our own lives.

Volunteer work somehow forces us to forget all those issues. There is something very humbling about volunteer work. It's sad to think that it takes seeing another person's struggle to put our own lives into perspective. It's like we can't see the forest for the trees. We are so focused on what's not right that we forget about what is right.

I think many people don't volunteer because they don't want that reminder. They make the excuse that they don't have time, they don't know who to contact, or they sent money so they shouldn't have to volunteer their time. Time is much more important to most of us than money. That's why we give money instead of time. If we can't find the time to help another human being then we obviously have our priorities out of alignment.

Let's make the time to help another human being.

Let's volunteer at a shelter today. It can be a homeless shelter, a shelter for runaway teens, a shelter for unwed mothers, or a home for children taken out of an unsafe environment.

Let's focus on helping others today, others that have nobody else to turn to.
Let's help others that have been abandoned by their families
Let's help those people suffering from mental illnesses that prevent them from working.
Let's help the single moms trying to raise children, work, and be both a mother and father.
Let's help the abused and the runaways.
Let's cross the tracks and hang out with the down and out.
Let's volunteer our most precious commodity, our time.

Let's volunteer at a shelter…just for today.

I'll bake cookies and deliver them to someone who wouldn't expect it.

It seems like baking is somewhat of a lost art. We've convinced ourselves that only the stay-at-home moms have time to bake. Grandmas don't really even bake anymore. We've gotten to the point that we'd rather work another hour than bake a meal for our family. And yes, I am extremely guilty of this as well. My kids didn't even know I knew how to cook for years. If we needed cookies for a school function, I would stop by the local bakery and buy our cookies. It's so much faster and more convenient.

It's also much more impersonal. This is tough to admit but very true. Buying cookies and delivering them just screams "You aren't important enough for me to spend time and precious energy baking. My job is much more important than you." I've noticed both at work and home how surprised people are when someone brings a food item that is "home-made." It's special, unusual, and unexpected. It is met with "oooohs" and "ahhhhhs" as if it were a rare commodity. I've seen children totally amazed to find home baked cookies available at a friend's house.

Let's dig out a recipe book, blow off the dust, and actually bake some cookies from scratch.

Let's think about someone who would never expect to receive these cookies; maybe someone who doesn't get out much, or a widow with a family, an old friend you haven't seen in a while, or maybe someone you have been at odds with.

Let's put all our love into baking these cookies, keeping in mind who they are going to.
Let's think of how happy this special person will be to receive our gift.
Let's make sure someone knows they are worthy of our time.

Let's find a beautiful way to present our "gift."
Let's take the time to arrange them in an appealing way and deliver our gift without expectations. It's all about the act of giving.

Let's bake some cookies for someone that would never expect it...just for today.

I'll listen to a different type of music.

Since we're working on our adaptability to change, let's try a different type of music today. We have a tendency to get stuck in ruts and then as we get older we find it more and more difficult to get out of those ruts. We have our certain type of music and we think all other music is unbearable. If you have a teenager, you know just what I'm talking about. The reality is there is value in all music. There is a message, there is a rhythm, and there is a story. Our challenge is to get past our own beliefs and actually try to determine the message in the music. This won't be easy for some of you but it will be good for you.

Let's switch the radio station today.

If you normally listen to classical, let's switch to rock today. If you listen to country on your way to work, switch to gospel. If you listen to Christian contemporary, switch to opera. Instead of oldies, let's try "Pop." And if you are home cleaning for the day, crank it up and really listen. Here's a challenge—let's listen to whatever our teenagers are listening to for the day and ask them to explain it to us.

Let's open our mind to the lyrics, the tone, and the individual instruments.
Let's try to determine why so many people love this music that we've chosen to exclude from our lives.
Let's close our eyes and feel the rhythm.
Let's listen to the story being told in the lyrics.
Let's be open to new ideas and a different viewpoint.

Let's listen to a different type of music...just for today.

I'll visualize myself achieving my goals.

Those that know me well will be shocked to realize this was one of the last pages I finished for this book. I've always been known to be very driven and goal oriented. Maybe I was saving the best for last. The first step to accomplishing any goal in life is to first visualize yourself achieving it.

I loved the movie "Space Jam" where Michael Jordan is depicted as a child that wants to be a basketball star. A song is played someplace in the movie with a verse that says "If you can dream, you can be it. If you can believe it, there's nothing to it." I think the key to this concept and reason so many people do not accomplish their goals is because they can't really see themselves in the vision. They can see the goal but they can't see themselves as the star of the show in that visual image.

Let's visualize ourselves achieving our goals.

No matter what the goal—let's see ourselves accomplishing it. Let's imagine every detail—how it will feel, how it will look, others who might be there. If it's losing weight let's really see ourselves as smaller, healthier people. Let's see ourselves eating like a slim person. Let's envision ourselves with more energy.

If it's writing a book—let's see our name on the cover. Let's visualize the speaking engagements that will come with being an author. Let's see our name on the best seller list at the local book store.

If it's becoming the owner of our own business—let's see ourselves at chamber of commerce and business owner association meetings. Let's visualize how we will greet our customers and what our store front will look like.

Let's see ourselves as the star of this production, front and center in the middle of this visualization. Let's visualize our families supporting us and friends cheering us on. Let's visualize what it will feel like to accomplish this goal. Let's take the first step to accomplishing our goals in life. Let's see it so we can begin to believe it. Then let's burn that image deep into our subconscious so we don't lose sight of it.

Let's visualize ourselves achieving our goals…just for today.

I'll remember the people that shaped me into the woman I've become.

Here's a newsflash for you, we didn't get where we are today all by ourselves. Sure, we worked hard. We overcame tremendous obstacles. We endured more than our share of broken hearts and bruised souls. But there were teachers along the way, lots and lots of teachers, hundreds of teachers (maybe thousands). They taught us through their actions, sometimes without saying a word. They showed us what we wanted to become as well as what we didn't want to become. Some of our teachers were in our lives for a moment in time while others have been an integral part of our entire life. Some of the lessons were extremely difficult to learn while others we absorbed instantly.

Let's remember all those people that shaped us into the women we've become.

Let's take a walk down memory lane and think through the lessons taught and those we actually learned. Let's think through the lessons we had to endure over and over again before we actually figured it out. Even the negative experiences contributed to molding us into stronger, more determined women. Let's say a silent thank you for the opportunity to learn (even the ones that hurt) because without them we couldn't be where we are today. Let's remember the many teachers, counselors, friends, and mentors—the ones we never met and the ones we see every day.

So many people contributed to our development—let's remember them, privately or publicly…just for today.

I'll spend the night in the back yard.

I have been so fortunate to have had the opportunity to own a home in the country. We owned property with no trees as well so we had a clear view of the sky. Then we had a giant trampoline in the back yard that was a perfect place to sleep under the stars. I remember the absolute joy in the kids' face when they ran in the house to propose sleeping in the yard for the night. They were so excited at the prospect that they couldn't hold it in. Out came the sleeping bag and flashlights and the imaginations went wild with anticipation of the stories they'd tell all night. Of course we never got any sleep. By the time the friends came over, five or six kids and mom and dad on the trampoline was not conducive to a comfortable nights sleep. But oh, did I love the view and the vastness of the sky!

Let's sleep in the backyard tonight.

It doesn't matter if you live in town, you can still sleep in the yard. The view may not be as great, but the effect will be close.

Let's drive a few miles outside of town if possible and find a place to lay our sleeping bags or blankets.
Let's bring someone we want to spend time with.
Let's not plan on sleeping.

Let's enjoy the stars and sky.
Let's remember how small we really are in comparison to the universe around us.
Let's enjoy the quiet and the beauty of the sky.
Let's wonder out loud about the heavens and our future.
Let's enjoy the show nature has provided.

Let's sleep in the backyard…just for today.

I'll remember that all things worth having are worth working for.

I learned at a very early age that the only way to get ahead was to work harder than others; as a young adult working harder turned into working more. When my friends were out having fun I was working my second job. As a new mother I not only worked full time but went to college full time as well. I had goals and dreams that weren't going to get accomplished all by themselves so having fun wasn't an option in my mind.

Hard work is good for us. We appreciate the outcome when we know we've given our all to achieve it. I know people who have had everything provided for them and their level of appreciation is very low. On the other hand you can tell the people who worked hard for what they have—they take great pride in whatever "it" is, they display it, and they take care of it. Whether it's spending the day weeding the garden, studying for an exam, painting a picture, or writing a book—hard work is good for us emotionally, mentally, and physically.

Let's work hard today.

Let's give our all to whatever we do. Although I'm not at all a theologian, I think the Bible tells us to work at whatever we are doing as if we are working for God. It's unfortunate but true that for some of us it would make a noticeable difference if we cleaned the house for our family than if we cleaned the house for someone more important. And there are those of us that coast through the day at work wasting time—would our behavior be different if we recognized who was watching our actions. Let's give 100% today.

Let's remember that all things worth having (now or in the future) are worth working for…just for today.

I'll remember God created me…and He doesn't make mistakes.

Sometimes I look in the mirror and feel nothing but UGGHHHH! I wonder why I can't look different, why God gave me such humongous thighs, why my hands are bigger and I'm taller than most men. I wonder why I'm not more personable, more generous, more mechanically inclined. I wonder why my life seems so hard in comparison to others—why I make so many mistakes. I'm never happy with who I am and am always wondering what God was thinking when He created me.

God doesn't make mistakes. Look at nature and it's obvious. Every flower, every limb on every tree, every plant and animal has a unique and special purpose. When we walk through a forest we don't pick each tree or rock apart. We take in the whole experience acknowledging the very special purpose of each and every plant and animal in our presence. When we look at a sunrise we don't proclaim "it should have more blue or red today." No, each and every day we look in awe as God wakes up the world with His gentle alarm clock. God made us too. It seems we forget that. Man has tried to dictate how we should dress, live, eat, and believe. And unfortunately we have bought in to those beliefs and spend our days wishing we were something we never will be.

Let's remember that God made each and every one of us.

He made us perfectly the way we are for a very specific reason.
He directed the look of our face and feelings of our heart.
He created our size and shape for his perfect purpose.
He placed us where we are just as He placed the squirrel in the forest.
He gave us specific talents and skills for a unique reason.

There is a perfect purpose and plan for you. How can you possibly be unhappy knowing that?

Let's remember God doesn't make mistakes…just for today.

I'll take a meal to an elderly person.

I know some of you are probably really great at doing this periodically. Others have probably never done it unless it was a sick or recuperating relative. The elderly in our country really get a bad rap I think. They have so much wisdom and experience to offer but we just think it doesn't apply to us. They have memories that are far better than any book yet we'd rather watch television. They are more often than not left behind to fend for themselves, even after giving their time for our country. They thought they'd be able to live on their pensions and social security only to find it's barely enough to eat. Instead of being angry at how slow they drive we should be in awe that they still drive. We need to place the elderly higher on the value chain.

Let's take a meal to an elderly person today.

It might be someone from church or someone down the street.

Let's cook a healthy meal and prepare enough extra to take to someone else.
Let's make sure it's something that can be refrigerated just in case they can't eat it all.
Let's be cautious of the spices—I hear it gets harder to digest as we age.

Let's wrap it in a dish that will force us to pick it back up.
Let's call ahead and let them know we are bringing dinner.
Let's plan on staying a few minutes and visiting, learning, and experiencing life through their eyes.
Let's make sure they feel valued and appreciated for what they have already contributed to this world.

Let's listen as they talk and really learn from their life.
Let's invest some time in this relationship.
It isn't just about the food; it's about the time spent and the acknowledgement that you care.

Let's take a meal to an elderly person…just for today.

I'll spend an entire hour in the bathtub.

I remember visiting my older brother and as he showed me around his new home I couldn't help but notice a big Jacuzzi tub in the bathroom. His wife is a middle school teacher and he said in his Texan drawl "I don't know what those seventh graders have got but they flat kick Elizabeth's butt every day. She comes home after work and sits in that tub every night for an hour with a glass of wine." I envied her then and I still do today. I envied her because I can rarely sit in a bathtub for more than ten minutes. I don't care how sore, tired, or mentally exhausted I am, I just can't sit still that long. I get in the tub with every intention of enjoying it and then my mind starts filling up with all the things I need to be doing. I think over-activity is a disease. I hope it can be cured.

Let's sit in the bath tub today.

Let's plan on an entire hour in the tub.

Let's put some candles in the room and bubbles (or bath beads) in the tub.

Let's bring a couple of magazines if necessary to keep us busy.

Let's lay out a towel, turn off the phone, lock the door, and escape.

Let's let everyone else in the house know they are not to bother us unless someone is dying.

Let's make it nice and hot (unless it's hot outside) and then replenish it as it cools off.

Let's get a bottle of wine, put it on ice, and have ourselves a little mono-party.

Let's spend an entire hour in the bathtub...just for today.

I'll go to a remote location and scream as loud as I can.

Sometimes we all just need a little release. My children are a classic example of this. My normally soft spoken daughter will occasionally run through the house screaming for no apparent reason. She's not angry and actually as soon as she is done screaming she starts laughing. It's like there is this pent up energy that just has to be released. There's nothing wrong with needing a release. We endure a great deal of stress every day—it has to come out somehow. Screaming is a nice alternative to some of the other ways it could come out—i.e. yelling at our kids, hitting people, eating…you get the idea.

Let's scream today.

We don't have to scream at someone and we don't have to scare the neighbors to death. If you live in close proximity to others then go to a remote location, outside the city limits if possible. This is difficult to do for some people. We've been programmed to maintain self control so letting it all out seems foreign to us. It would be a good idea to take a friend along because we will probably need some coaching and encouragement to let it all out. Or, hey, here's an idea—how about a screaming party. Get five or six friends and go out to the country to scream. You can even bring the kids along—they will think it's a blast! Let's take a deep breath and just let it out. Plan on the first time not being good enough—it's going to take a few times for you to really be uninhibited about this. Come on, it's okay to scream. It will feel good. Let's do it a few times. Let's get all that pent up frustration and negative energy out.

Let's go to a remote location and scream as loud as we can…just for today.

I'll handwrite a letter and send it via snail mail.

I believe letters are the easiest thing to put off. After all, we have email now and can fire off one or two liners when the mood strikes. Letters take more time and effort. They have to be at least one page long and that would probably take, huh, 15 minutes to do. And then there's the whole addressing the envelope and finding a stamp…we're talking 30 minutes now. There are so many other things we could be doing with our 30 minutes—watching a sitcom, reality show, or talk show on TV. Even if we do manage to get the letter written and in an envelope, there's the whole actually getting it to mailbox or post office. However did they get that accomplished before email?!?

I have letters written to me from 20 years ago. I don't have emails written a year ago. My letters are amongst some of my most prized possessions. I have letters from my parents, my friends, my siblings, and even a few old boyfriends. I have cards and letters from every significant event in my life. I have letters of congratulations and letters of encouragement, letters wondering how I'm doing and letters expressing I am loved and missed. I have no emails like that. My father, who died unexpectedly when I was 18, sent me a letter the day he died. I'm glad he took the time to write that letter and put it in the mail instead of watching TV.

Let's write someone a letter today.

Let's take the time to write a heartfelt letter someone may keep until the day they die.
Let's tell someone we miss them.
Let's encourage someone.
Let's write a note telling someone how proud we are of them.
Let's create and memorialize our feelings, thoughts, and activities.
Let's make sure to get it in an envelope, put a stamp on it, and actually get it to a mail box.

Let's handwrite a letter and put it in the mail…just for today.

I'll skip (no matter how foolish I feel).

I've tried it and you'll have to believe me when I say it is impossible to be 40+ years old and skip without laughing. I challenge you to try to skip with a frown on your face. Skipping is just a happy activity. If you aren't happy when you start you will be in the process.

My 18 year old daughter hates the idea of growing up. She forces me to stay young. We can be walking along Main Street and for no reason at all she'll put her arm in mine and start skipping, laughing, and dragging me along with her. I'm sure it's quite a site to the passersby but we don't care. We laugh and giggle like seven year olds. There is just something about skipping that immediately makes you feel carefree and full of laughter. We should all experience that feeling more often.

Let's skip today.

You can be assured it will make you feel foolish but who are you here to impress anyway?

Let's have some fun.
Let's be carefree.
Let's go arm and arm with a friend or our teenager.
Let's live a little.
Let's put a little spring in our step, get the blood flowing and skip down the street.

Yes, you will get a few looks but once they see the laughter on your face, they'll be envious. There is no law that says only seven year olds can skip. We can experience this carefree feeling any time.

Let's skip, no matter how foolish we feel…just for today.

I'll talk less and listen more.

God gave us two ears and one tongue for a reason. Why do we struggle so much with just closing our mouth and listening? Why must we feel so compelled to talk about ourselves or others? Do we think it makes us more interesting? Do we think our thoughts and words are more important than the next persons? Or are we just not comfortable with silence in a conversation?

The single greatest reason for miscommunication is our inability to listen. We try to multi-task or interpret what the other person is trying to say before they even get the words out. It's arrogant when you think about it to assume we know what the other person is trying to say—why not just give them the opportunity to say it. Not only do we not listen to people, we don't listen to the sounds around us. We miss the gentle whisper of the wind, the joyous sounds of children playing, the birds singing a song. We miss so much because we don't listen.

Let's talk less today.

Let's really get to know other people by allowing them the opportunity to speak. Let's listen to their words, their expression, their non-verbal as well as their verbal language.

Let's give someone else a chance to take center stage, to shine, to share a bit of themselves.

Let's be the one person today that makes them feel important by simply closing our mouths and opening our ears.

Let's listen to the sounds around us, the sounds of the house, the wind blowing through the trees, the birds chirping, and the children laughing.

Let's take the focus off ourselves and put the focus on everything and everyone around us.

Let's use our two ears and close our one mouth…just for today.

I'll pick a street and pick up trash.

I am appalled by litter. I remember pulling off the side of the road when a passenger threw trash out the window and requested they pick it up before we proceed. I can't believe people can be so lazy as to throw their trash out the window instead of taking it home and putting it in the trash can. There are trash cans everywhere—even the drive thru has a trash can now. Trash is a detriment to our environment and it just plain looks bad. We can make a difference today. We can do something good. It doesn't matter what tomorrow brings, we can do something today. There is a misconception that we can't make a difference unless we have a lot of money to give or a lot of time to donate. That just isn't true. We can make a difference each and every day.

Let's pick up trash today.

Can you imagine what the city would look like if even half the population took one day, picked a street and cleaned up the trash?

Let's pick a street and spend two or three hours picking up trash. We can wear gloves if necessary. Let's take plenty of trash bags.
Let's make a difference on this street today. We can pick another street some other day but today let's concentrate on one street.

Let's pick up anything that doesn't belong.
Let's fill up as many trash bags as necessary.
Let's make a difference today.

Let's pick a street and pick up trash...just for today.

I'll turn off the Television.

As a nation we have become overwhelmingly dependent on the television. It seems to control most homes' schedules and activities. Some research suggests American's watch an average of four to six hours of television per day. That means in most homes the TV is on in the morning before work as well as four or five hours after work. This means if I get off work at 5:30 pm, home between 6–7 pm (depending on the number of stops I have to make on the way home), the TV is on until well after the 10 pm news is over. If that's the case, I have to ask "Are we spending any time in conversation anymore?" I've read other material that suggests parents spend about 3.5 minutes per day in meaningful conversation with their children. Hmmmm…do we see a connection? The television has turned from a source of entertainment to a source of control.

Let's turn off the TV today, for the entire day.

Just one day without news, sitcoms, and reality TV is not going to kill any of us. If you have to record your favorite show so be it.

Let's eat a meal together and have actual conversation about our day, our feelings, our beliefs, our fears.
Let's spend the evening reading books or going for a walk.
Let's do the dishes together.
Let's play a board game or card game.
Let's call someone and give them 100% of our attention instead of 50%.
Let's enjoy the silence and peacefulness of not having 15 different voices in our home this evening.

Let's turn off the television…just for today.

I'll tell my parents "thank you for raising me."

Too many people are unappreciative of all that went into raising them. As a nation we have a tendency to blame our parents for everything wrong with us. It's their fault we are neurotic, not balanced, too strict, not strict enough, overweight, have an eating disorder, not successful enough—you name it and it's our parent's fault somehow. Instead of taking responsibility for ourselves as adults and "fixing" whatever it is we need to work on—we prefer to blame or parents.

Here's a news flash for you—we pretty much all come from dysfunctional families. The only difference is the level of dysfunction. There are a fortunate few that came from loving, supportive, two parent households. The key is they aren't the majority. Since I am a parent now—I realize I have made many mistakes. Try as I might I can still look back and find 1000 things I should have done differently with my children. But I did the best I knew how. My heart was always to do what's best. And although they may see things differently I struggled to provide "the best" for them. I believe all parents do the best they know how. It may not be as good as the person next door but they do the best they know how to do regarding their children.

Let's take a step back and give our parents the benefit of the doubt.

Let's trust that they sacrificed and did the best they knew how as parents.
Let's acknowledge the fact that they weren't given an instruction manual when we showed up.
Let's appreciate what they did right instead of focusing on what they did wrong.
Let's trust there was a reason God gave us the parent's He did.
Let's honor their viewpoints and beliefs.
Let's remember they will be gone too soon.

Let's tell them "thank you" for raising us…just for today.

I'll be still and know that He is God.

We sure have a tendency to get worked up over things don't we? We can't stand it when things don't go as we planned. The idea of not being in control of our own lives is maddening. And being in control of our own lives isn't good enough for us—we want to be in control of everything around us—the traffic, the weather, our kids, our spouse, our co-workers, and even our future. Whether it be with relationships, schedules, career, or family responsibilities we seem to stay in a constant state of frustration. We want it all, we want it our way, and we want it now. We mistakenly believe it is supposed to be our way.

Let's take a step back and remember who is really in control.

Maybe we wouldn't be so frustrated if we gave the power back where it belongs.

Let's quit fighting God's decisions and trust all things happen for our own good. Let's willingly give Him the authority he deserves and will take anyway.

Let's trust there is a bigger purpose behind it all than just to frustrate us. Believe it or not, it's not all about us—God doesn't sit up there in heaven and make it rain just to ruin our day.
Let's realize there is a bigger purpose in life than our individual happiness.

Let's have a reality check and give the credit and authority where it belongs.
Let's control what we can control and turn the rest over to the One that is really in charge.

Let's be still and know that He is God…just for today.

I'll leave all the lights on.

I've spent most of my adult life turning off lights. It's become as automatic as breathing. I think it started during our very difficult financial days when I tried to control any part of reducing costs that I could. And then it turned into an obsession. Of course I used the excuse of energy conservation as a reason for my obsession. Actually, it was all about control. If there is a light on and nobody has been in the room for 10 seconds I'm all over that light switch. My daily reminders to those around me include "The lights are on," "Did you turn out the light?" "Obviously, you aren't paying the electric bill." At different points in my adult life I've even gone so far as to put signs above the light switches as a reminder to everyone else (just in case I'm not there to do it for them or remind them). My battle with the light switch is only compared to my battle of the bulge. It's a losing battle.

Let's leave all the lights on in the house.

Let's try something different today. For one day resist the urge to follow some-one out of a room and turn off the lights. For those cringing now in the name of energy conservation—this is not about "wasting" energy, it's about mellowing out a little bit.

Let's not follow anyone out of a room today and hit the light switch.
Let's not tell anyone else to turn off the lights either.
Let's keep our opinions and reminders to ourselves today.

So what if the closet light was left on all day. One day of lights left on are not going to make a significant difference in your electric bill. Let's relax a little.

Let's leave the lights on…just for today.

I'll hit the snooze button once, twice, three times, oh well.

The toughest realization I ever came to was the realization that the world could and would go on without me. It didn't end when I got sick or otherwise incapacitated. The sun actually continued to rise, my employer didn't shut down the facility, the kids found their way to the bus, and the earth continued to rotate. It was difficult to acknowledge that I wasn't as important as I had hoped. I had spent my entire adult life taking care of everything and everyone around me. To realize it wasn't necessary anymore was overwhelming. I have to admit; once I overcame the initial shock it was a relief to not feel the pressure of the universe anymore.

The world can go on without you today too.

The earth will continue to rotate, the kids will be fine, and the job will still be there along with all the paperwork you left yesterday. Go ahead, hit the snooze button. You need your rest. You work way too hard. Sleep in an extra 10 minutes for once. Or spend the time snuggling with your spouse—you never get to do that! What the heck, hit the snooze button a second time. You know what, turn the alarm off and just sleep in as long as you need. I'm not suggesting you make a habit of this but one day isn't going to hurt anything.

Hit the snooze button today, as many times as necessary…just for today.

I'll make an inside fort and play in it.

I remember when I was young and my favorite thing to do on a rainy day was to build a tent inside the house. My mom would throw a sheet and some blankets over the table and my brother and I would grab our flashlights and pretend we were in the wilderness.

When my children were small they enjoyed it just as much. They were so excited they could hardly contain themselves as I set up their tent while they went and gathered all the things they would need for a "camp-out." They packed up favorite toys, favorite blankets, sleeping bags, pillows, coloring books, flashlights, and of course, food. It made a rainy day seem like heaven to them. The simplest things in life excited them more than anything I ever bought at the toy store.

There is something to be said about simplifying our lives.

Let's make an inside fort and play in it today.

Kids are not required but they are helpful to fulfill this activity. If you don't have any of your own see if you can borrow a friend's children. This activity can also be done with a spouse or a couple of girl friends. If you are doing this with grown ups I'd suggest a manicure set instead of toys. And instead of food bring a bottle of wine.

Let's pretend we are on a camping trip.
Let's cover the dining room table with blankets.
Let's grab a flashlight, some blankets and pillows and prepare to tell our favorite ghost stories.
Let's turn off the cell phones, unplug the land lines and pretend we are in the wilderness.
Let's play one of those sound CD's of the wilderness or a thunderstorm for the mood effect.
Let's make an inside fort, block out the outside world, pretend we are in the wilderness with no modern conveniences.

Let's make a fort inside and play in it…just for today.

I'll sit down and think about the "good times."

Many people that know my past are surprised that I have turned out to be a normal, functioning human being. As is the case with many people my life hasn't been easy. But I have a choice—I can focus on the positive or I can focus on the negative. I have been blessed in this life to be filled with good memories that counter the bad ones.

I have memories of my brother and I being mischievous and coming up with the most unusual things for our step siblings to do to join our "club." I have memories of my older brother "protecting" me from boys when I was a teenager. I have memories of camping with my three siblings and spending lazy summer days in the mountains. I have memories of swimming with my mother at the city pool after work late at night the summer before she died in a car accident. I have a million memories of parties and dancing with my best friend from high school. And then, of course, I have all the memories of my kids growing up—the best memories of all and the greatest blessing I've ever received. Those memories tell me my life hasn't been bad at all.

Let's remember the good times of our life.

Let's focus on all that has gone right.
Let's see the glass as half full today.
Let's remember all those wonderful times and stories and places that we've had the amazing opportunity to experience.
Let's conjure up those memories that are tucked away.
Let's blow the cobwebs off and relish in those events.
Let's go ahead and share these memories—it will probably bring a tear or two to your eyes but that's okay.

Let's sit down and remember all the good times…just for today.

I'll sneak into the McDonalds play place and cover myself with the balls.

Who said just because you have given birth to children (or are old enough to) that you can't have fun anymore? I remember when my children were young I loved hearing the laughter in their voices as they played in the play place at McDonalds. They couldn't care less about the food—it was all about playing. They used to beg me to play with them. Back then my entire focus seemed to be on making sure they were clean, safe, fed, and healthy. I had no time (or so I thought) to think about fun. "Come on mommy, play with us" they would beg. Of course, back then I was too grown up and mature to play. After all, I was a "mother." Now that they are grown, I want to play in the play place.

Let's play today.

I know all the posted rules at McDonalds say if you are over a certain height you are not allowed in the play place. We have to think about why the rule was created and if it really applies to what we want to accomplish. I'm guessing it was created for the children's safety—they didn't want older kids to be in there that might be rough with the little ones. Now that is a good reason for this rule. However, we aren't going to hurt anyone. We are responsible adults.

Just for today let's sneak into the play place. You may want to borrow a friend's child if you don't have one that meets the height requirements—you'll be less obvious that way. When no one is looking, sneak into the ball pit and bury yourself. For those of you that strictly follow the rules, think about this—what are they going to do if they catch you—arrest you?!? I doubt it. The worse thing that can happen is they will ask you to leave.

Go on, live a little, play a little, have a little fun...just for today.

I'll imagine a world with no anger.

I know it's a stretch of the imagination but I like to think it's possible to envision a world with no poverty, anger or hatred. Anger is responsible for virtually every crime, every miscommunication, and every wrongful act. It starts with a hand gesture and turns into road rage. It starts with a scowl and turns into a beating. It festers, builds, and ultimately explodes and controls. It affects everyone in its path. Left unattended, ultimately, it infects—like a cancer, it ravages the body and ultimately the soul.

Call me optimistic, maybe even unrealistic but I can see a world with no anger.

Just think of it…instead of the undesired hand gesture by the driver behind you; a waving hand and smile takes its place. Instead of the woman screaming at you for accidentally taking "her" parking spot, you receive a chuckle and "I needed the extra walk anyway." Instead of the scowl of your co-worker, you receive a genuine heartfelt greeting. Instead of being angry with your significant other for neglecting to run the errand you asked, you are thankful they made it home safely and blessed with yet another day in their company.

We contribute to the anger in our society. Every time we demonstrate anger, we affect another human being. We affect and we "infect." Just for today, let's control our anger and envision the entire world without it. Let's smile and wave when someone honks at us while driving. Let's take the time to greet someone that is obviously unhappy.

Let's imagine a world with no anger…just for today.

I'll leave the dishes and enjoy life.

Dirty dishes seem to control our lives sometimes. We think we can't go to sleep until the dishes are done. We can't watch TV until the dishes are done. We can't spend time with family or friends until the dishes are done. Who are we really doing the dishes for anyway? Does our spouse really care if the dishes aren't done for one night? How about the kids? Yeah, right. Does anyone really care except us? Who came up with the idea that the dishes had to be done before we could enjoy life anyway? Are those dishes really going to grow legs and walk away if they go unwashed one night (hey, that might be a good thing)?

Maybe it stems from fear—fear that someone will see our dirty dishes and label us a "bad mother, wife, person." Or fear our kids will go to school and tell all their friends that the dishes weren't done and SRS will be sent to our home as a result. Let's be realistic here. You and I both know the only time the kids are going to complain is if there are no clean bowls for cereal. And if you really think they have nothing more important to talk about with their friends than your cleaning habits, you are living in a fantasy world. Lastly, why would we care what the neighbors think—they are after all, neighbors.

Let's let it go tonight.

Let's enjoy the time with our family and friends. Let's spend the time reading a good book. If your mother in law shows up and has a problem with it tell her it is so much more important to you that you have the time to truly visit with her than to spend it washing dishes. Let's not let the dishes control our lives or even our evening. Let's not worry about it. Let's spend our time with our family.

Let's leave the dishes and enjoy life…just for today.

I'll live in the moment.

This particular thought seems so obvious and overused. Upon further investigation however, I realized it is so rarely practiced. We spend hours, days, weeks, and entire years living everywhere but in the present. We think about what we need to do tomorrow, we plan for our retirement, and we stay angry over events in the past.

We are so busy living in every other moment that we miss the precious moment at hand.
We are so pre-occupied with wishing we had more than we do that we miss the value and beauty of what is right before our eyes.
We are so busy thinking about tomorrow's work that we miss the conversation our child is trying to have with us right now.
We miss so many moments because we are consumed with moments we have already experienced and those we may never have.

Just for today, only today, let's live in the moment.

Let's experience today with no thoughts of tomorrow.
Let's bask in every single moment provided, right here and right now.
Let's experience this moment to the absolute fullest—everything about it, the smells, the sights, the sounds, and the feelings.
Let's experience every detail of this moment.
There may be no tomorrow and we can't change yesterday; let's live in the moment as it is provided.

Let's live in the moment...just for today.

I'll have faith in myself.

I truly don't understand how such capable, accomplished people can have such little faith in their own ability. We act like we own the world but deep down inside we don't try something new because we are afraid we will fail. We don't start that new business we've always dreamed about because we are afraid it won't work and then what will everyone think of us? We don't go on a diet because we've failed so many times before it just isn't worth it to try it anymore. We don't enter that 10K we've always dreamed of because we don't think we can get in shape in time. We don't go back to school because we think we are too old. Of course all the while we say we don't do these things for other reasons—don't have time, don't have money, don't have support—you name it. The reality is we don't have faith.

Let's have faith today.

Let's take a look at our resume and all we have already accomplished. Is that not proof enough that we are capable? We only get one shot at this life, do we want to spend it full of regrets. Let's make and plan and do it.

Let's break the dreams into chunks and get busy working toward it—one step at a time. Before we can run a 10K we have to be able to walk a mile. Before we can start a business we have to do a little research and come up with a defined process and plan. Before we can go back to school we need to call the admissions office and see what it will take.

Let's have a little faith—you have already accomplished so much. If we can't have faith in ourselves, who can we have faith in? There is so much more waiting for us. There is no-one stopping us but ourselves.

Let's have faith in ourselves...just for today.

I'll trust my gut.

One of the most important lessons I ever learned was to trust my instincts. Unfortunately it took me almost 40 years to learn this lesson. For whatever reason, I constantly doubted or was unable to identify that gnawing feeling in my stomach when it came time to make a decision. I let others talk me into or out of things that had I trusted my own instinct I would have never done. I was concerned that I didn't have enough data, was being too rash, not giving the other person a chance when the reality was God equipped me with a sensor that alarmed like crazy but I didn't understand what the alarm meant. You have that sensor too. You are equipped with a built in right/wrongometer that too often you don't trust. You let others talk you out of what you know is right or wrong.

Let's trust our instincts today.

Let's have the confidence to know we have the right answer within us.
Let's filter out everyone else's advice and seek the answer that is already there.
Let's not be afraid to do what we know is right even if others disagree.
Let's not give in to insecurity.
Let's have the confidence to know that everyone else doesn't know what is right for us.
Let's listen to that still voice in the pit of our stomachs telling us the right thing to do.

Let's trust our gut…just for today.

I'll go barefoot.

My fourteen year old son never has shoes on. Of course, with a size 15 shoe I'm all for him saving those expensive shoes for when he really needs them. I always have to tell him to put shoes on when we go somewhere. If he had his way I think he would go barefoot to school, church, and anywhere else he needed to be. It's as if someone is cutting off his oxygen supply to force him into a pair of uncomfortable dress shoes.

I used to think the reason he resisted shoes was a result of all that country living he experienced growing up. Then I realized it was a common trait of most kids. It made me wonder why. I think it's because they love the freedom of being barefoot. Like clothes, shoes confine them and take away their freedom. Shoes seem to make kids feel trapped and bound up. We tell them they need shoes on to protect their feet but the reality is we are limiting their experiences. We are preventing them from feeling the sensation of fresh cut grass, sand, mud, and water. We are limiting their freedom with a simple pair of shoes.

Let's go barefoot today.

When was the last time you felt mud between your toes or walked in a puddle of water? Let's take a step back and actually feel nature all around us. Let's remember why they love to be barefoot. We torture our feet all week with shoes that I swear a man must have designed. Let's give those feet a rest and go barefoot today. If you don't normally do this your feet may be a little sensitive but bear it out. Let's experience the feel of grass under our feet. Let's walk in a water puddle. Let's kick our shoes off at the park and play in the sandbox. Let's feel life all around us.

Let's go barefoot...just for today.

I'll buy a bag of groceries for someone.

There are so many people in need. They are all around us and we don't even see them. I remember in my final year of high school I was already living on my own with my best friend. We both worked full time and went to school full time. For whatever reason, to this day, I feel guilty about the fact that we used to routinely steal toilet paper from the local truck stop. We both worked there so our meals were free but we were so broke we couldn't afford the "necessities" of life. I'm sure nobody had any idea how bad off we were. They assumed our parents were providing for us.

I also remember during this same time period I was on the basketball team and was sick. I didn't have the money to get any medicine. One day I found a $20 bill in an envelope in my mailbox. I still don't know who provided that money but I remember it and how much I appreciated it.

Let's buy a bag of groceries for someone today.

It might be an elderly person that is having a difficult time living on social security or a single mother struggling to feed her children. Let's pay attention to the people around us. If you don't know someone, hang out at your local grocery store and your opportunity will soon make itself known. Let's let them get to the checkout line and then take over the payment. Let's go to the store ourselves and buy a bag of milk, bread, meat, and vegetables and take them to someone we know can use it. Let's think outside our own issues and help someone else get through the week.

Let's buy a bag of groceries for someone…just for today.

I'll choose the important vs. the urgent.

Each day we are bombarded with demands. We are pulled in a 100 different directions and it seems every task on our list is urgent. The kids need to be at soccer practice, we need to make a dish for the church potluck, we have a report due for work, neighbors are coming over for barbeque, the house needs to be cleaned, the dog needs to go to the vet, we need to pick up the dry cleaning, the bills need paid, and then we need to fit time somewhere in there to take a shower and go to the bathroom. Everything is urgent. Everyone *needs* us and our time (or at least they think they do). In the process, we are frazzled and exhausted from all the activity.

Today let's focus on the important instead of the urgent.

Is the dry cleaning more important than spending time with our family? Our days are numbered; we may not get a chance to put it off for tomorrow. Let's spend our time on what is most important instead of on who screams the loudest. Is the church potluck meal coming before our own family's meal? Is that report for work more important than watching the sunset with our spouse? Can we do a better job at delegating or getting others to help us so we can focus on what is really important? Let's take a deep breath, step back, and really prioritize all the activities we have on our plate. Let's focus first on what's important and don't let the urgent cloud our judgment. Let's make a choice today.

Instead of letting others run our lives, let's choose the important vs. the urgent...just for today.

I'll work towards my goals instead of someone else's.

I've spent the majority of my life working toward somebody else's goals. If you aren't self-employed, you are also spending your day working towards somebody else's goals. Every business in existence started first with a dream. That dream turned into a plan and that plan turned into a reality. There are times when our personal dreams are in alignment with the job we have. Let's say we've always wanted to be a hairdresser so we go to work in somebody's salon. That's great if we have a job that helps us achieve our goals. Oftentimes however, we settle—we settle for a job we don't necessarily enjoy or we work for someone with values that don't align with ours. We tell ourselves it's better than nothing and we just stick it out. We lose sight of the fact that we have goals and dreams too—goals and dreams that we can't work on if we are giving our best twelve hours a day to someone else.

Let's focus on our goals today.

Let's schedule time to work toward our goals.
Let's create a plan to achieve our goals.
Let's dare to dream and plan our own future instead of giving our best energy towards somebody else's dreams.
Let's see our dreams coming to fruition.
Let's put ourselves first today.
Let's envision accomplishing this goal.
Let's imagine every detail of what that accomplishment looks like, feels like, and tastes like.
Let's get hungry for our own accomplishments and stir that fire up to get us moving.

Let's work on our own goals instead of somebody else's…just for today.

I'll live life wide open.

We've all heard the term "life is short" but too many of us don't take it to heart. Sure, when a loved one dies unexpectedly we start thinking about our own mortality but we don't make any permanent changes as a result. We spend a week or two thinking about the person and how sad it was that their life was unfinished but we don't like to make changes in our own lives. We go right back to living our daily rat race and we make a mental note that "someday" we are going to (fill in the blank).

Let me make this loud and clear—LIFE IS SHORT. We need to live life as if every day were our last day. We never know when that day will be. If we want to make a difference in this world we have to do it today. If we want someone to know how we feel about them, we need to do it today. If there are things we want to accomplish, we need to start today.

Let's live this life we are given today to the absolute fullest.

Let's enjoy every moment.
Let's make a difference in someone else's life today.
Let's not just dream, let's do.
Let's slow down and enjoy this day.
Let's tell our loved ones how we feel about them.
Let's help those people we've always wanted to help.
Let's take a step toward accomplishing our goals.
Let's watch the sunrise AND watch the sunset.
Let's play with our kids.
Let's not be afraid of anything or anyone.
Let's live this day as if it were going to be our last.
Let's explore and learn.

Let's live life wide open…just for today.

For more information about the author, how you can live your life "just for today", and other products please visit our website at www.maripeck.com

978-0-595-40726-2
0-595-40726-9

CPSIA information can be obtained at www.ICGtesting.com
Printed in the USA
LVOW07s0148010914

401799LV00002B/620/P